Sensing the Enemy

Sensing the Enemy

LADY BORTON

The Dial Press
DOUBLEDAY AND COMPANY, INC.
GARDEN CITY, NEW YORK 1984

Published by The Dial Press

Copyright © 1984 by Lady Borton

Manufactured in the United States of America

First printing

Library of Congress Cataloging in Publication Data
Borton, Lady.
Sensing the enemy.
1. Refugees, Political—Vietnam. 2. Refugees, Political—Malaysia. 3. Viet-
namese Conflict, 1961–1975—Personal narratives, American. 4. Borton,
Lady. I. Title.
DS559.912.B67   1984   959.704'3   83–15364
ISBN 0-385-27754-7

Designed by Judith Neuman

This book is published with the aid of two grants from the Ohio Arts Council,
which is hereby gratefully acknowledged.

 Ohio Arts Council **Individual Artist**
Fellowship Recipient/FY 1983

Ohio Arts Council **Individual Artist**
Fellowship Recipient/FY 1982

for
all our children

Kẻ thù ta đâu có phải là người.
Giết người đi thì ta ở với ai?

Our enemy is not people.
If we kill each other, whom shall
   we live with?

—PHAM DUY
   Vietnamerican Songwriter

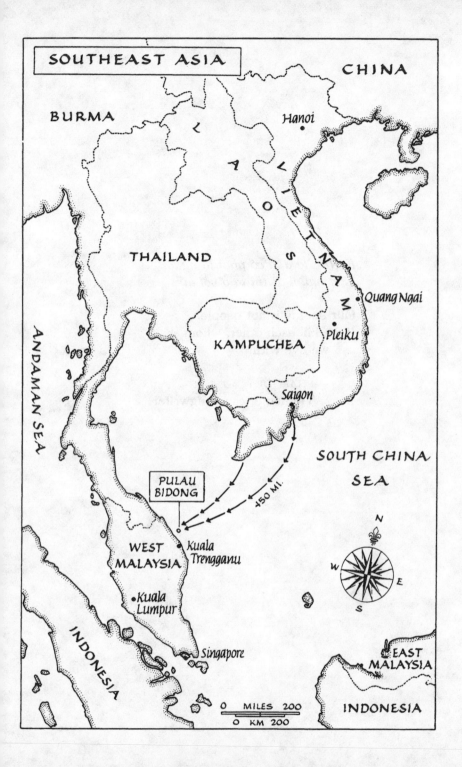

SOUTHEAST ASIA

CHINA

BURMA

Hanoi

THAILAND

V I E T N A M

L A O S

Quang Ngai

Pleiku

KAMPUCHEA

Saigon

PULAU
BIDONG

450 MI.

SOUTH CHINA
SEA

ANDAMAN SEA

WEST
MALAYSIA

Kuala
Trengganu

Kuala
Lumpur

Singapore

INDONESIA

EAST
MALAYSIA

INDONESIA

N

W   E

S

0   MILES   200

0   KM   200

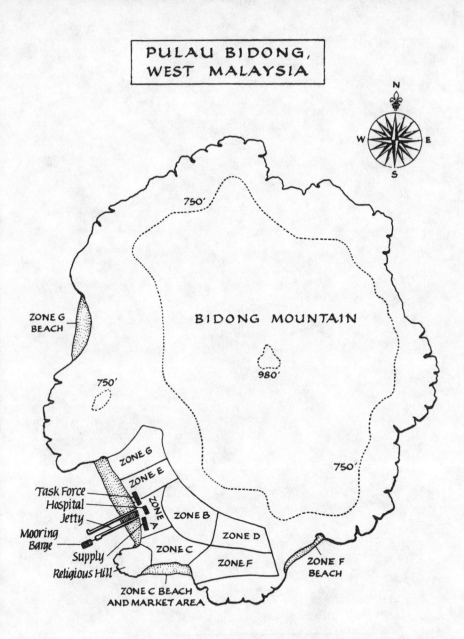

PULAU BIDONG,
WEST MALAYSIA

BIDONG MOUNTAIN

750'

750'

980'

750'

ZONE G
BEACH

ZONE G

ZONE E

Task Force
Hospital
Jetty

ZONE A

ZONE B

Mooring
Barge

ZONE D

Supply
Religious Hill

ZONE C

ZONE F

ZONE F
BEACH

ZONE C BEACH
AND MARKET AREA

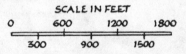

SCALE IN FEET

0   600   1200   1800

    300   900   1500

Sensing the Enemy

It was the summer of 1971, just weeks after I'd returned from the war in Vietnam. America seemed wild and frightening, brazen with freeways. I was driving from Washington to Boston when I lost my way on an interstate near New York City. The July heat was heavy that day. Passing buildings pulsed with neon. Signs and exits raced by. Trucks loomed up behind me before they roared past, blowing their air horns.

Then, on both sides of the highway, as far as I could see, stretched a graveyard—stone after gray stone. Rain started to fall and I slowed down. Thunder shook the air and with each crack like an exploding mortar, a sense of panic welled up from somewhere deep inside my chest. The tombstones went on and on like rows of parading soldiers. It rained harder and I turned up the radio. On the news, the President advocated more funding for the war in Vietnam.

The rain pounded with the savagery of a monsoon, the wake from each passing truck breaking over my VW Bug and thrusting it toward the guardrail. For a split second the wipers flicked the waves away and once again I saw gravestones, row upon endless row. The radio announcer listed the body count for American soldiers but disregarded Vietnamese. The tombstones and spires and mausoleums darkened, closing in; the road and the water grayed until panic washed over me.

I pulled off onto the shoulder of the road, and wept.

1

A Volcano

The day was muggy, breathless and hot, alive with small black gnats. A sturdy wooden fishing trawler loaded with pack rations pulled away from the jetty in Kuala Trengganu, Malaysia, and headed for the river channel leading to the open sea. It was February 14, 1980.

I sat on the trawler's deck, watching the oily, mud-colored river slide by the scarred red and white hull. Rotten pineapples floated in the murky water. The Malay captain puffed on the stub of a hand-rolled cigarette as he steered the vessel away from an oil tanker hard aground on an approaching shoal. He grunted, nodding at a fishing boat wrecked on the opposite reef. I looked more closely and saw the boat's wooden ribs rising like dragons' fangs from the surf.

"Vietnam!" The captain yelled over the engine noise as he pointed at the wreckage. With his forefinger he wrote "150" on the steamy cabin window. Talking in Malay, he placed the backs of both hands in front of his face and made a forward arc as if diving, then threw back his head and flailed his arms. He made his body go limp like a corpse.

As we entered the channel, the trawler's wake struck the Vietnamese boat in which, it seemed from the captain's gestures, 150 people had drowned. Waves slapped the wide eyes painted on the boat's bow to ward off threatening spirits. The breakers jostled loose a hull plank and beat it against the ribs. Water lapped around the engine, which lay exposed inside. Near the engine bobbed a child's rubber sandal.

"Vietnam," the captain yelled again. He pointed across the sea, then to the Malay town sprawling along the river. "MRCS," he shouted, referring to the Malaysian Red Crescent Society, the Malaysian equivalent of the American Red Cross. Gradually, by means of gestures, Malay phrases and a few halting words of English, the captain conveyed that his vessel, *Red Crescent 2,* had itself once been a refugee boat.

The engine accelerated, and *RC 2* rose and plummeted through the great swells that forced their way into the river. Waves struck the hull, splintering into slivers of light. Spray beat against my face as I gazed out over the open water to our destination: Bidong Island. Its volcanic silhouette loomed over the South China Sea.

The wind was blowing clouds across the sun. The sky turned somber, and the distant silhouette changed to a surly gray against gray. Pulau ("Island") Bidong, the largest refugee camp in Malaysia, housed thirteen thousand Vietnamese boat people in the same amount of space as the valley farm on which for years I'd lived alone. I was to be its health administrator for six months. Now, I was having second thoughts as I watched the island come close.

The roll of *Red Crescent 2,* the vibration of her engine and the taste of salt spray made me think of another boat on whose decks, years earlier, I'd learned to walk and run.

Erma, the thirty-six-foot sloop my family owned when I

was a child, had also been used by "boat people." At the end of World War II in Europe, sixteen Estonians fleeing the Russians had sailed that sloop without power across the Atlantic, tossed and rolled and pounded all the way. Hearing of the Estonians' arrival at Norfolk, my parents drove down from Washington and bought the beleaguered *Erma*. The planks in her hull had sprung leaks. Bilge water sloshed over the floor; algae coated the cabin walls. My parents scrubbed and hammered and painted, slowly transforming *Erma* into the pleasure boat on which I spent my childhood summers.

When I was three years old, I loved to sit on *Erma*'s water barrel, which rested on its side in a cradle. I loved the feel of its wooden ribs curved against my thighs. A few years later, I began to wonder how sixteen people could have survived two months on the open sea in such a small boat. I tried to imagine myself as one of the Estonian children, squabbling with my brothers over a daily half cup of water while the sea rose ominously between the floor boards.

Sometimes, when I was older and my brothers were tormenting me, I'd look down and think that maybe some day my hands would be useful. At home, I loved to twirl the living-room globe, feeling its raised longitudes ripple under my fingertips as the earth gradually slowed and my index finger settled on some faraway spot. I'd look it up in the *World Book* and imagine myself working there, far beyond my brothers' reach.

Now, as I tasted the salt spray thrown from *Red Crescent 2*'s bow, it occurred to me that I was descended from "boat people," Quakers who had sailed to America three hundred years earlier.

RC 2 was drawing nearer to the island and to the generation of boat people I'd soon meet. A hum emanated from the base of Bidong's volcanic cone. Spots of blue at the volcano's base gradually focused into plastic huts clinging to cliffs. A dark mass on a beach became an active market; dots in the surf turned out to be children. Loudspeakers shrieked names and numbers. When *RC 2* rounded a point and nosed toward a jetty, the air thickened, weighted with the heavy odor of rotting cabbage.

I stood up as the first mate came forward. He tossed a rope to Vietnamese men standing on a rusty barge moored at the end of the jetty. The men belayed the line to a post as the captain threw the engine into reverse.

"Okay-*la!*" he shouted, the cigarette wagging on his lower lip. He waved to me. I waved back and jumped ashore.

Suddenly I felt cast adrift, as frightened as the first time I'd jumped from *Erma*'s deck into a terrible, vast, throat-clogging sea. I looked around. Vietnamese longshoremen, their bare shoulders glistening with sweat, thronged the rusty barge. Their voices seemed harsh. Indifferent to my arrival, they unloaded huge baskets of cabbages that already were disintegrating into an odorous brown slime.

A Western woman and a Vietnamese man approached. The man, who was in his mid-forties, had graying hair that bristled from his cowlick. This added a youthful air to the formality with which he introduced himself in Vietnamese as Dr. Cung, the camp leader. Suddenly I felt embarrassed. In the hasty language review I'd done before leaving home, I'd forgotten to study pleasantries; I bowed and mumbled and bowed again as I lamely thanked him.

"And I am Monika, the radiographer with the tuberculosis program," the woman said with a German accent. Tall and gaunt, she wore no makeup. Like me, she was in her late thirties. Fine blond curls radiated like static from her face, and below her blue eyes were dark hollows that looked as if they'd been smudged with charcoal.

As Monika and Dr. Cung led me down a long pier, I scanned the beach up ahead and saw a flux of people all with straight black hair. Behind them, blue plastic huts overlapped one another like the shards of a kaleidoscope. Bidong Mountain rose above the people and their shanties, bare and forbidding, its orange slopes stripped of foliage and bristling with stumps. Voices. Everywhere voices and, overhead, loudspeakers screeching a list of new arrivals. People were as thick as tropical air, as restless as waves, people eddying around a beachside warehouse and streaming along paths.

"It's almost suppertime," Monika said at the end of the pier as Dr. Cung bowed and took his leave. "Will you like to wash up?" Leading me along a camp path, she fended for space among the press of bodies as she led me to a tin shed with an Asian squat toilet. I shuddered at the sight of a four-inch hole with two raised foot rests. I'd forgotten. Of course I'd used an Asian toilet countless times, but I was out of practice. This toilet reeked like my outhouse at home in July, but that privy's steady perch required no feats of aim.

Monika pulled back another gunnysack curtain. I looked inside and saw puddles glimmering on a floor made of rough lumber slats. There was no shower or tub, only a dipper floating in a drum of water.

"Will you know how to use?" Monika asked.

A few minutes later, we returned along the twisting paths to supper. My shoulders brushed against walls made of gunnysacks and cardboard. The roofs were constructed from jungle saplings draped with sheets of blue plastic. The floors were sand. A stench rose from gray muck oozing between the huts; the odor hung over the narrow paths with a heaviness that made me reel.

In one hut three men squatted on a bed made of lashed bamboo canes. They scooped rice from their bowls with chopsticks. Flies buzzed around the rice. The men called out to us in friendly voices as their wooden sticks clicked against the plastic bowls.

A girl with hazel eyes pushed past. *"Bà Mỹ!*—American woman!" she said, pointing. She made no distinction between Monika and me.

"Hello! Hello! Where do you go?" a boy chanted in English. He wore a Pittsburgh Pirates T-shirt a size too large.

"Em đi đâu?" I answered, asking him the same question.

"Trời ôi!—Oh, heavens!" the boy said, stopping for a moment before the crowd pushed him on. "That one can talk."

I felt embarrassed: a freak with white skin and copper-colored hair, which was kinky at that—a monster who loomed a head taller than everyone else, even the men. I'd forgotten that I'd be the awkward subject of constant remarks, my every action noticed and thoroughly discussed. I began to sweat as I followed Monika to supper, recoiling when my damp arms slipped against the greasy skin of strangers.

The "Coconut Inn," where MRCS staff ate meals, was a corrugated-roofing lean-to in a row of huts. A Vietnamese woman stirred a wok full of cabbage over a fire pit near a bamboo table. She was about thirty-five, with a soft face that had features curving one into another like the petals of a wild pasture rose. She lifted shreds of cabbage in her chopsticks and dropped them into the waiting beak of a white duck at her feet. The duck swallowed and opened its bill.

The woman dished up some cabbage and served it to Monika and me along with rice and egg drop soup. As she set spoons and forks before us, I introduced myself. Her name was Anh, which means "Flower." When I asked for chopsticks in Vietnamese, Flower laughed in recognition, tilting her face toward one shoulder. She responded in a flurry of incomprehensible chatter as she left, but soon she returned with chopsticks and a second bowl of soup. From its taste I could tell she'd added an extra dash of fish sauce.

The stench that clung to everything and the thousands of voices reverberating like the frenzy of cicadas on a summer night made me feel queasy. I ate only out of politeness, and even then I felt guilty. I knew the islanders had had no fresh fruit, vegetables, meat, or eggs in over a month and that they restlessly awaited distribution of the newly arrived cabbages. As I nibbled, children stood behind the low corrugated wall that separated the Coconut Inn from crowds pressing along the path. They stared with almond eyes, watching me eat.

After supper, Monika took me inside the hospital, a two-story rough lumber building surrounded by palms. A single tree arched through a hole in the roof, its fronds drooping over the corrugated sheeting. The hospital reeked with that camp smell—a mixture of stagnant water and stale urine—but tinged with the biting odor of medicinal alcohol. It had electricity but no running water. Four wards plus the operating and delivery rooms were downstairs. The laboratory, pharmacy, Monika's room, and mine were on the second floor.

Mounting the stairs to my own quarters, I opened the door to a room as stark as a nun's cell. The plywood walls were blank and the room was bare of furniture except for a cot, desk, and water bucket. Louvered windows opened to the sea. As soon as Monika left, I closed the door, grateful for my own space and, within that space, solitude.

2
Madness

Tôi có người yêu chết trận Pleime
Tôi có người yêu ở chiến khu "D"
Chết trận Đồng Xoài
Chết ngoài Hànội . . .

I had a loved one killed at Pleime
I had a loved one in War Zone "D"
Killed at Đồng Xoài
Killed in Hànội . . .

A soft soprano voice rose from the beach as I lay on my cot that first night on Bidong. For some minutes I listened to her plaintive song, allowing homesickness to wash over me. Then a squeaking sound jarred me. I rolled over to see a rat poking its head through a hole at the base of the opposite wall. The rat was huge. Its nose twitched. When it started toward my bed, I slapped the floor. The rat veered, running straight up the wall and out the window. I took one of my shoes from under the bed and wedged the toe of it into the hole, then closed all the window louvers.

Immediately the room became airless. Sweat seeped from my face and neck. It dripped from my chin and ran off my arms while from the hole came the soft sound of teeth gnawing on leather. I rapped the wall, and the chewing stopped, but it began again, louder. I beat on the floor but the rat persisted. Furious with defeat, I retrieved my shoe and opened the windows. After that, the rats came and went, sometimes as many as ten at once. Every time one of them entered, my blood turned gray.

I lay back down and concentrated on the repetitious breaking of the surf, each wave a painful reminder of how far I'd come from home. I tried to picture my valley farm in Appalachian Ohio, thinking that maybe I could draw imaginary hills around me. But whenever I closed my eyes, I heard the sea gather and sigh. The loudspeakers blared a list of people leaving the next morning for the States. I longed to go with them, then felt guilty for wanting to run away.

In 1967, thirteen years before I found myself on that cot on Bidong, I was teaching at a Quaker school in Philadelphia. I watched the news every evening when I came home. It was the first year I'd lived alone and the only year, including my childhood, that I'd ever had a television. Night after night Vietnamese refugees streamed across the flickering blue screen. Their voices chattered incomprehensibly; their faces were anguished. Their cries seeped into my imagination, echoing there during the day, and their faces stayed with me deep into the night.

Those evenings I tried to concentrate on my classes, but as I corrected papers, I saw my students' faces: earnest, momentarily carefree, perplexed. The boys, almost eighteen and already husky, were facing the war; the girls worried about losing them to it.

Two years earlier, when U.S. Marines landed in Đànẫng, one student had persuaded me to join a silent vigil in front of the Pentagon. As a child, I'd often visited the Pentagon with a friend's father; then it was an irresistible playground of waxed corridors perfect for sliding. But when I stood silently outside as an adult, its massive façade seemed impenetrable.

I attended other demonstrations with growing dissatisfaction. When some of my students left for Vietnam, I grew haunted by the futility of teaching teenagers who would soon be shot. I came to understand that I would be a conscientious objector rather than kill.

Increasingly I felt drawn toward working in Vietnam, yet I worried that relief agencies relying on U.S. Government money had become adjuncts to the military. One group that refused those funds was the American Friends Service Committee (AFSC), the same Quaker organization for which my father had directed relief programs in Germany after World War I. For a year I badgered the AFSC to send me to Vietnam. Finally, in early 1969, I left on a two-year assignment as Assistant Director of the Quaker refugee programs in Quảng Ngẫi, a provincial capital in central Vietnam.

When I returned to the United States two years later, I set to writing a novel about the war. Yet, whenever I tried to make up Vietnamese characters, the memories of real people from Quảng Ngẫi intruded. Years of grappling with this novel turned into grim endurance. I ended my six-year relationship with Eric, a Quảng Ngẫi teammate, because he wanted us to have children but I needed to write. After that I lived alone on our valley farm. By then I'd found a job driving a school bus. Months passed. Then it was years. I abandoned farm projects and stopped having morning coffee with other school bus drivers. More and more I stayed at my desk.

The fall of 1979 was bleak. The leaves rotted. The woods, pastures, and meadows turned into soggy brown. When winter came with savage force, I closed off the rest of the house and hibernated in my attic study. As I worked, I threw discarded pages onto the bed next to my desk. At night they crinkled beneath me as I slept. Night after night I awoke from a fitful sleep into bitter darkness, turned on the lamp, and, wrapping myself in quilts and scarves, engaged the monster my book had become. Yet the harder I worked, the more stilted were the pages I produced.

One cold, gray Saturday in December, when the surrounding hills resonated with the sounds of hunters, I let that writing go. I'd been up much of the night before, trying to create on paper a refugee camp like one I'd visited in Pleiku. Sitting at my desk, I gazed at a black-and-orange weaving that hung over the bedstand. The cloth had been made by a Montagnard woman whose tribe had abandoned its hunting grounds after American planes sprayed the defoliant, Agent Orange.

As I looked at that fabric, I saw it stretched once more on a loom in front of the woman, who wore a similar weaving wrapped around her hips. Her bare, shriveled breasts trembled every time she threw the shuttle. The weaver's three-year-old son lay naked at her feet; with his bloated belly, he looked like a butternut squash lying in the dirt. His glazed eyes stared from beneath black hair fringed with burnt orange, a symptom of advanced malnutrition.

In my attic study, I looked away from the weaving and began to cover pages with revisions full of penciled arrows. I typed and penciled, retyped and repenciled. Finally I threw the papers onto the bed. Why bother? Who would care?

I picked the pages back up, willing myself to focus one more time. For my children, I thought—for the children who ride my school bus, for the children who rode my bus in Quảng Ngãi, for all the children on all the buses, everywhere.

Then, deep in my bones, I realized I couldn't prevent their war, just as I hadn't stopped the war for those students I'd taught in 1967.

I heard gunshots and looked across the brown fields to the far ridge. Men carrying shotguns against orange vests appeared over the hilltop. They were dragging a carcass. Hunters, I told myself, but then I heard the *chop-chop* of a helicopter, saw it graze the hill, watched it unload men in green fatigues. They carried M-16 rifles. Other choppers landed, disgorging men. I could see the soldiers' faces: high school boys I'd taught, toddlers from Quảng Ngãi, neighborhood kids, the riders on my school bus. They began shooting. I saw a face blown away. I saw a body spin and tumble.

Everything in me stopped.

I let my hands fall, useless, into my lap. I lowered my head onto the papers that cluttered my desk, feeling hot tears run down my face.

I lived in a stupor for four or five days after that Saturday in December. I couldn't read, not even the local paper; I couldn't even write my own name. Every morning I ran my bus route, but between routes and in the evenings, I settled into an old blue rocker, my feet on a pulley from *Erma*. For hours I stared at photographs on the living-room wall. I looked into the framed faces of people I'd known in Quảng Ngãi, each one captured in a moment ten years before, and wondered where their lives had taken them.

There was Truong, a three-year-old who had toddled around the Quảng Ngãi hospital grounds, toting a bottle filled with yellow liquid—either tea she'd fetched for her paraplegic mother or urine she'd emptied from her mother's catheter. The child's home was a grass mat under her mother's cot. Like the ward, the mat smelled of urine. In the living-room photograph, Truong covered giggles with her pudgy fingers.

There was the photograph of Bo, a monk, the clown of that same paraplegic ward. He'd been shot in the back while tending bougainvillaea in the monastery garden on Buddha Mountain. In the photograph he looked bewildered.

And the old lady butcher in the Quảng Ngãi market and the younger woman who sold ducklings from her conical hat. And the old fortune-teller, who wore a white *aó-bà-ba* pajama suit and squatted on the corner of Phan Bội Châu and Route 1, his *Chinh* coins and Chinese text nearby.

And there was the photograph of Toi, the thirty-year-old quadruple amputee prima donna of the Quaker Rehabilitation Center. Presenting her stumps, Toi would recite the Center's news as her prosthetist strapped each artificial limb into place. Once helped onto her legs, she would strut around the Center, knees squeaking, hooks swaying, her grin toothless.

I knew the end of Toi's story. Initially she'd been shot by American soldiers during the Mỹ Lai massacre, though not fatally. Other bodies in the mass grave shielded hers. After learning to walk on artificial legs, Toi returned to Mỹ Lai, where she was wounded in the stomach by crossfire during an attack by Vietcong revolutionaries. Following treatment in the Quảng Ngãi hospital, Toi returned once more to Mỹ Lai, where she died during an American bombing raid.

Now, as I sat there rocking, gazing at the faces which for years had haunted me, I gradually abandoned the need to create fictional characters. Little by little, watching the dogs asleep by the fire, I was able to accept that my life would be enough if I did nothing more than drive my children safely to school and share farming with neighbors.

I emerged from that week, frail and tremulous. I closed off my attic study and began once more to see to farm chores. In the evenings I went out to a local pub with other bus drivers, who taught me to shoot pool.

Adrift and empty, I reached out to friends. Eric, the Quảng Ngãi teammate with whom I'd lived, suggested I apply for the Bidong position. Within a week of our phone conversation, I decided to go. I felt I needed to shake my introspection. I wanted distance from books and I thought the six months might provide perspective. Or maybe, if I were honest, I'd say I fled.

Neighbors agreed to keep up my fences and to bring in my hay; the school gave me a leave of absence. One brittle January day after my departure date was firm, I sat with the dogs in front of the stove and wondered how within a week I could find someone to take care of my house and animals.

I heard a knock.

In ten years, no stranger had ever walked into the valley. The man at the door was of slight build, with copper hair and a copper beard. When he said he was looking to board two mules, I knew from his gentle accent that he'd come from Kentucky.

"I'd like to," I said, "but I'm leaving for six months."

"I need a place for six months," he said. "You interested in renting?"

I showed him the living room with its peeling wallpaper and took him into the kitchen, where I pointed out the ladder to the attic study. We went outside to the spring gurgling from the hillside and then across the snow-covered pasture to the natural gas well fizzing in the ravine. As I introduced him to the goats, the old mare, and the cows, I relaxed in the knowledge that the valley, the farm and everything living there would be safe.

One week later, on a morning clogged with snow, I closed the front door behind me and stood on the porch, ready to leave. Shouldering my knapsack, I glanced at the dogs, who lay side by side on the porch, their chins on their paws. Each one fixed me with a morose gaze.

"Stay," I said, touching their ears. I turned and walked into the unbroken drifts. Ahead of me lay a half-mile walk to the road, where I was to meet my ride to the airport. I couldn't bear to look back as I climbed toward the giant ridgetop oak that for years had spread its branches over my school bus. "Stay," I called into the wind, which stung my face.

"Stay. Stay," came the echo from the hills.

◉ 3
Tết, the Year of the Monkey

My first morning on Bidong, I awoke with a feeling of dread.

It was the day before Tết, the Lunar New Year. I lay on my cot and stared at the bleak walls. Rolling over, I glanced at the floor littered with rat droppings and rolled back. As I stared at the ceiling, I remembered that during Tết nobody works. For three days everyone would be feasting with loved ones.

Suddenly I felt desperately alone. I considered going out for a walk, but cringed as I imagined voices chanting, *"Bà Mỹ! Bà Mỹ!*—American woman!" Shyness crept over me, and along with it came the choking wish to be back home.

Later that morning an Indian in his late fifties appeared at my door. Against his generous paunch he carried a conch shell the size of a concertina. Delicate lines like staffs of music curved from the conch's rose-colored whorl. The Indian set the shell on my desk so that its music flowed toward me. He smoothed his hair, which was combed straight back in silver furrows. His pudgy face broke into a smile as he introduced himself as Mr. Narayanan, but he spoke in such a lilting flow of English that I had to ask again for his name.

"Just call me Uncle," he said. "I handle supplies on the island."

From his pocket Uncle withdrew five booklets of snapshots. He showed me photographs of one son's wedding, a flurry of pastel saris. Next he displayed booklet after booklet with photographs of his "adopted sons and daughters." In each snapshot, he stood surrounded by Vietnamese men and women, his supply warehouse with its red crescent moon in the background.

Uncle offered to take me on a tour of the camp. As we left the hospital, I noticed an old woman in black satin trousers and a peasant blouse. She was placing incense on a small Buddhist altar. The enclosure, hardly larger than the palm trunk it leaned against, had been built in memory of a man killed on that spot by a falling coconut. A fragrance of burning spices rich in cinnamon floated from the altar. The old woman knelt and bowed, her clasped hands pulling inward, her neck stretching forward as she swayed. Before her on a platter lay a chicken, plucked and naked, its wings crimped back, its neck and beak craning toward the Buddha.

I heard shouts and looked down the beach. Two small children dressed as dragons jumped from behind a boat wrecked on the sand. Other children crowded about the dragons, which shook their cardboard carton heads. With a great clattering, the monsters locked their horns made from ration tins. They snapped cardboard jaws with strings dripping from charcoal teeth. Encircled by children, the dragons lunged and dodged, swirling their tails of blue-striped plastic as they turned down a path and disappeared into the camp.

Uncle and I followed the dragons and the children into the labyrinth.

Uncle led the way between houses and over ditches filled with sludge. I kept losing sight of him as he pressed through the swarming crowd. Children inside the shanties spotted us. They ran under the men swinging in hammocks and around the women tending cooking fires.

"Hello, hello," they chanted.

They trod on the heels of our flip-flops and hung on our arms as if our limbs were the rungs of a jungle gym. From everywhere came the buzz of voices, and above that hum, the blare of loudspeakers announcing the distribution schedule for Tết rations.

We passed an old woman displaying three cans of cola atop a cardboard carton much as a youngster at home might sell sidewalk lemonade. Nearby, two girls washed clothes in a plastic tub, which they emptied into a ditch. A man with a helicopter tattooed on his arm urinated into the same trench.

The sun beat down, and Uncle's dark skin began to glisten. We held our noses as we passed a toilet block, which was a series of rough lumber cubicles perched on stilts. The islanders flushed the toilets by aiming a hose at the hole. The toilets reeked. The day before, there'd been no water to flush them; feces piled up out of the holes and over onto the raised foot rests.

"Phew!" Uncle said, fanning his nose. "High tide."

I followed him, tiptoeing through a latrine site from a year earlier when 43,000 people had lived in the camp. That was before the hospital had been built, and before the refuse barge or the toilets. Until 1978, Pulau Bidong had been an uninhabited jungle yet by this day in early 1980, 65,000 people from 692 boats had landed here. Ten thousand would arrive during my six-month stay. Walking with Uncle I felt dizzy from the stench and the heat and the children who clung to me with the tenacity of leeches. I reminded myself that during the war I'd visited camps with far worse conditions, but even so I felt overwhelmed.

We climbed past a graveyard, the only part of the camp empty of people. Crowded with tombs, it was fenced off by bamboo branches. I paused for a moment, studying the Buddhist mounds and Catholic crosses, which rose like specters through the wavering shrouds of heat. At the base of one tomb, flowers trembled in the breeze. The stems had been made from bamboo twigs, the petals from noodle wrappings.

On the next ridge, we stopped to wipe our foreheads near a helicopter pad used by VIPs. Small heaps of trash dotted the knoll, indicating that it had been a while since chopper gusts had swept it clean. With a stick, Uncle cleared a space in the sand. He sketched a map of the camp.

"*Đẹp quá.*—Beautiful, Pa-*pa,*" said a ten-year-old girl with buck teeth. She stretched forward to watch, leaning her cheek against his arm. He added an approaching boat and she laughed, covering her mouth.

"Seven zones, A through G," Uncle said, dividing the map into sections. "You're here in Zone F, at Pulau Bidong International Airport."

I glanced up from the map and looked over the camp concentrated on one third of a square mile. The camp was blueness: blue plastic, blue-striped plastic; blue-checked plastic; houses made from blue plastic stretched over lashed jungle saplings; palm trees with blue plastic, cardboard and gunnysack houses clinging to them. To one side lay the cramped green of a farmer's plot, but mostly the view was blueness broken only by snaking paths and ditches oozing slime.

I thought of a walk I'd taken a week earlier, just before

leaving home. Snow had pattered against the few desolate leaves still clinging to their branches. It burned my cheeks and crunched under my boots as I climbed to the far ridgetop with the goats and the dogs. The goats trod on my heels; noses to the ground, the dogs wove patterns around my footprints as they sniffed for rabbits. From that ridgetop I'd looked back over the stark and empty whiteness toward the farmhouse tucked into the valley's cove and distinguishable from the expanse of snow by a tiny square of yellow light.

Now, on the airport ridge, I felt I was suffocating as more children ran up, clinging to me. A girl with a double harelip nuzzled my forearm. She carried on her hip an infant clad in only a T-shirt. The baby's head was shaved except for a tuft of hair on the soft spot above his forehead.

The children surged around Uncle as he started down the hill. "Pa-*pa!*" they shouted. His silver head bobbed over their black ones; their golden hands grasped his thick, dark arms.

Uncle led me and the children down to the black market on Zone C beach. The beach front looked like a carnival with stalls of lashed bamboo canopied by blue-striped plastic. A woman wearing lipstick and eye shadow ran her fingers over a remnant of green brocade that seemed to please her. She looked away as she suggested a price. The merchant, a small woman in a faded cotton blouse, snorted and refastened a pink foam roller she used as a barrette. Nearby, a woman with a pockmarked face served *phở*—a spicy noodle soup—to two men whose high cheekbones made them look like brothers. Across from her, a man sold rubber sandals and watches. He was barefoot and wore a digital watch with a calculator on it.

According to Uncle, Malaysian fishing boats had brought the black market goods during the dark of night to Zone F beach on the back side of the camp. Before daybreak, Vietnamese laborers unloaded the merchandise for Vietnamese entrepreneurs, who were mostly of Chinese ethnic origin. The entrepreneurs hid the goods in their huts before distributing them to the vendors, again mostly ethnic Chinese, who in turn sold them in the market.

At one stall Uncle removed a hundred-dollar greenback from among Australian, British, Canadian, and American bills displayed like playing cards arranged by suit. I was amazed to see four more one-hundred-dollar bills, plus an assortment of twenties and tens, as well as gold and jewelry. Uncle told me that before they left Vietnam, the boat people transferred any assets into gold, jewels, or Western currencies, only to find that upon arrival on Bidong, they were required to turn their assets over to Malaysian guards for safekeeping.

Some new arrivals slipped their valuables past the guards, while others received money hidden in packages mailed from the West. Although this gold and cash entered illegally, the islanders changed it openly on the market for Malaysian ringgit, which was Bidong's currency. Later I learned that MRCS allowed overseas relatives of boat people to send cashier's checks, which MRCS deposited and paid out to the recipient family at the rate of one hundred ringgit (fifty American dollars) per month. Islanders due to leave . for resettlement to another country took extra ringgit to the black-market money changer, who converted these savings into one of her four Western currencies.

"She's not allowed to have those bills," Uncle said, nodding at the money changer. "Sometimes the Malaysian guards confiscate them. Watch. We'll make her squirm."

He waved the hundred-dollar bill he'd picked up, then pocketed it. The money changer ranted in Chinese, her gold teeth snapping. When her hair slipped out of its bun, she twirled it around her forefinger and stuffed it back into a knot at the nape of her neck. Her hands, on which she wore jade rings, fluttered. She bowed when Uncle replaced the bill.

Uncle moved away from the money changer's display. At a nearby stall he removed a can from a tier of rationed sardines. The vendor smiled when Uncle returned the tin. She wore her hair wrapped in a circle on top of her head as is customary among women from the North of Vietnam. In fact, her rationed sardines were worthless because no one could eat them. They made people vomit.

"Ah ha!" Uncle said angrily, seizing a lone can of rationed baby milk from behind the sardines. "That's *my* milk. They're always stealing my baby milk and selling it on the black market."

The saleslady grimaced when Uncle walked off with the can. Holding the milk tin under his arm, he moved into the milling crowd. He passed an old woman with one good eye and one empty socket. With gnarled fingers, she poked at a speckled squid that had eyes glistening with slime. At the next stall a teenage boy picked up a shaving mirror and admired the new coarse hairs on his upper lip.

A Malay in a flowered sarong approached. "He's a Vietnamese refugee," Uncle said as we passed a booth selling cut-off jeans. "Used to be a famous Saigon nightclub singer. Now he's the best on Bidong." Like other shoppers, the singer waved to Uncle.

"Here!" Uncle said, tossing him the tin of milk. "For your baby!"

It was clear to me as we walked through the camp that everyone knew Uncle because everyone came to him for food. Answering greetings from young and old, he led me back through the maze of lanes to his supply warehouse at the foot of the jetty.

"I'm head of Supply," Uncle said proudly as we stood near cabbages piled taller than his height. The outer leaves were a slippery brown and the air was heavy with their stench.

"And the other divisions?" I asked. "I know some of them, but not all."

"Nine more," he said, ticking each off on his fingers. "Education. Administration. Engineering. Language Interpretation and Translation. Security. Labor Recruitment. Social Welfare. Sanitation. Now that's eight. Where is number nine?"

"How about Health?" I suggested, raising an eyebrow.

"Yes, of course," he said, laughing. "How could I forget. Each has a head like me and you but also each has its own Vietnamese leader and his workers."

"And who chooses the Vietnamese leadership?"

"The Vietnamese."

"And how are the workers recruited?"

"Recruited? There is no recruited. All men work. Two days a week they must give. Some give much more, but two days they must."

Gradually, as we spoke, the Vietnamese governing body became clear to me. Distinct from the MRCS structure, of which I was a part, the Vietnamese administration consisted of the camp leader, his assistants, the division heads, and the chiefs of the seven residential zones. For ration distribution, islanders were grouped by their arrival boats with the captains continuing as leaders on the island.

"Well," Uncle said as he swung open the heavy warehouse door, "come see my palace."

I felt nauseated by the building's compressed heat and by the rank odor from broken bottles of *nước mắm*—a sauce made of raw fish that has decayed on a bed of salt. After my eyes had adjusted to the dim light of the warehouse, I noticed that the barnlike building was stacked to the ceiling with cartons containing ration packets—each with enough rice, noodles, peas, sardines, chicken, salt, and tea to feed three people for one day. In addition, the building housed rolls of blue plastic sheeting and balls of pink plastic twine for hammocks, plus monthly allotments of onions, garlic, fish sauce, firewood, mosquito coils, sanitary napkins, and toilet paper that was a startling pink.

Later that afternoon, from my room in the hospital I watched the Vietnamese supply staff distribute ration packets along with a special Tết dole—for each family a cabbage, a quarter of a watermelon, and several mandarin oranges. The cabbage, one of the few vegetables that can survive tropical transport in large quantities, would be for most families the only fresh food in a month; the oranges and watermelon were an unprecedented extra to honor the holiday. As I looked at the maelstrom of people surging against guard ropes that separated them from fruits and vegetables, I thought of the tiers of produce in the supermarket at home.

Without question, the Year of the Monkey was a Tết of lean feasts on Bidong; there were no traditional cakes made of sticky rice stuffed with sweetened green beans, no morsels of pork, no plum wines. Still, singing and dancing and impromptu dragon duels invigorated the camp. And, as it turned out, I had no time during Tết to feel lonely.

"Let me polish that belt buckle," Uncle insisted. Once again he'd stopped by my room, this time to invite me to supper with his friends. This was my first visit to the home of a Bidong family.

"It's useless to polish brass in salt air," I said.

"It's Tết. Toothpaste will shine it."

A half hour later, Uncle returned, laughing at his discovery that the buckle was engraved with the image of Virgo, her hair flying.

"I polished with pleasure," he said.

Uncle led me along the jetty beach. I stepped over empty cans with rusty, serrated edges. A wave riding up on the beach lifted the carcass of a rat, carrying the dead creature farther up onto the shore. As the surf receded, the rat rolled back over onto its bloated belly, and its claws sank into the sand.

We turned away from the water, onto a narrow path between shanties and climbed all the way up to the edge of the settlement. The huts we passed smelled of wood smoke, noodles, and cooked cabbage. Outside one shanty an old man was tying minnows to a strand of pink hammock twine stretched between two palms. The drying minnows hung down like silver clothespins.

"Hello, hello, where do you go," his toothless wife called in English from the hut. Her voice was festive. In a wok she sautéed more minnows that must have been caught near the jetty. Each morsel sizzled as she turned it, filling the air with the sound of spattering grease and the aroma of fresh fish.

"We're going to eat Tết," Uncle answered.

"You must eat your fill, Pa-*pa!*" the old woman answered in Vietnamese.

The house where we ate supper that night was home for two parents, the paternal grandmother, and twelve children. It was a little larger than my nine-by-twelve-foot room in the hospital. The roof was blue plastic and the walls were made from cardboard cartons. We sat on the edge of a bed built of lashed bamboo and ate off a slightly higher bamboo bed. In the dusty light, I could just make out on the hut's only shelf a yellowed photograph that might have been fifty years old. As far as I could tell, it was the family's only keepsake brought from Vietnam. In the photograph a man and woman, each wearing a brocade robe, posed on wooden chairs with arm rests carved into dragons. The woman held a pouting toddler. Other children in brocade robes stood to either side of the adults.

The father of the Bidong family sat with us while his wife and two eldest daughters served rice and cabbage they'd prepared over a fireplace fashioned from ration tins filled with dirt. The other ten children played outside. The women sat down, except for the grandmother, who hovered over the fire before joining the table. Her hair was receding, but she had all her teeth, which were painted a shiny black, as had been customary when she was young.

The grandmother laughed, flashing her beautiful black teeth as she lifted a sliver of cabbage with her chopsticks and deposited it in my bowl. "More food for health," she said. Her chopsticks worked constantly as she tended Uncle and me.

For dessert the daughters presented fresh apples that had been imported from New Zealand and smuggled into the black market. They were crisp and pleasantly tart.

"This my life goal," the father said in heavily accented English as he held up a sliver of apple. He wanted to know if he'd be able to raise such fruit in America after he joined his brother in Casper, Wyoming.

He rinsed instant-coffee jars with tea to clean them and then filled each one. "Excuse me, Pa-*pa*," he said, "but Supply tea not fine like I choose to welcome you at Tết." With one hand he gestured at the small room lit by a piece of string clamped over a cola can filled with kerosene.

"My house poor but here we rich in friendship. Drink for health and happiness in the Year of the Monkey!"

It's Tết, 1970. In Quảng Ngãi, a province capital of the South, the rocket launchers and rifles are quiet.

There's an uneasiness about this silence: everyone waits for it to split apart. Today people also whisper tales of two brothers from the opposing sides who met this very morning at the Quảng Ngãi airport. Normally the airport is held by Saigon soldiers during the day and by Vietcong revolutionaries at night. The brothers, according to the tale-tellers, sat down together and shared tea.

As is customary during Tết, I visit friends, sip tea, and exchange New Year's greetings. I stop by to see Ngo, an unemployed builder. A Buddhist altar set overshadows the room, which is home for his family of eight. A small table laid with teapot and cups awaits visitors. Nearby are special Tết cakes made of glutinous rice and sweetened green peas.

Ngo speaks of a tea that Vietnamese emperors prized. Since the vines of this variety spiraled too high into the treetops for the servants to climb and pick them, the emperor's staff trained monkeys to harvest the crop. They rewarded the monkeys that brought back the best selection of tea leaves with an extra long draft on an opium pipe.

Once the monkeys had collected the tea (and their opium), court chefs fed the harvest to a horse. They slaughtered the horse as soon as the tea entered its stomach. Then they removed the leaves and dried them. It was expensive tea, for not only did the servants train monkeys and sacrifice a horse but they needed a plentiful supply of opium, too. These prohibitive costs made this tea a delicacy reserved for the emperor alone.

Ngo tells this anecdote as he rinses cups with tea before filling them. "I wish I could offer you some of that special tea," he says, smiling. "But now I'm a poor man without work

and can share only very ordinary tea with you as we cele-
brate the Year of the Dog."

"More tea, *Con Út*—Last Little One?" the mother of
twelve on Bidong asked me. Her glossy hair was twisted into
a bun and held in place by two black-lacquered sticks.

Her daughters giggled. In answer to their mother's earlier
inquiries about my family, I'd admitted I was "the last little
one," knowing I'd opened myself to teasing. "There's another *con út!*" the oldest daughter had said, pointing to her
mother and then to the yellowed photograph with the pouting toddler. "She's spoiled, too."

"What do you think?" the mother asked as she refilled my
tea jar. "Are we spoiled?"

Later, as Uncle and I were leaving, she took my hand once
more. We stood near the hut's one shelf. "You must come
back and join our family," the mother said, bowing. The
kerosene lamp sputtered and brightened. For a moment, I
saw on the mother's face the same pensive look I'd noticed in
the photograph.

"Miss Lý! Miss Lý, come quick!" Bạch, the Vietnamese
hospital manager, interrupted breakfast the next morning,
leaning over the asbestos half wall that separated the Coconut Inn from the camp's main path. "It's that American," he
said.

"I thought we just finished with him," I said. Already, on
my second day, I'd been besieged with problems. The pharmacy was out of tuberculosis drugs, the operating-room ster-
ilizer had broken, and a visiting American journalist had
insisted on telling me how to run the hospital—all before
breakfast.

From the hospital entrance, I could see the American

standing in a crowd of Vietnamese at the far end of the
hallway. He was in his late twenties. A scar cut down his right
cheek to the edge of a downy mustache. Earlier he'd told me
that when he was ten and playing war, a friend had acciden-
tally slashed his cheek with a garden stake.

"Look at this mess," the journalist said as he kicked cigarette butts on the hallway floor. He picked up a ration wrap-
per, crinkled it and pushed the wad at a man with a drooping
eyelid. "Throw this away," he said. Drawing spectators the
way an electromagnet attracts iron filings, the visitor strode
into the maternity ward, a narrow room with ten beds; the
crowd accompanied him as if it were attached. I followed.

"Clean this up," he said to a nurse, waving his pencil at the
night table next to a mother's cot. With one arm the mother
drew against her breast a newborn son, who wore a knit cap
and tiny yellow mittens.

"It's disgraceful." The journalist kicked over a cola can
under the woman's bed. It toppled and a yellow puddle
spread over the rough boards, releasing the smell of urine.
The mother blanched.

"Don't let it worry you," I said to her in Vietnamese. I was
standing behind the journalist.

He spun around. "They're going to America. They can't
live like this."

Jerk! I thought, feeling my face redden. How do you think I
lived in Vietnam?

"Please," Bạch said, "we're not *in* America yet."

"I thought we'd settled this earlier," I said coldly.

"We didn't settle anything," the journalist said. "What's
there to settle? If these people are going to America, they
had better clean up their act."

"Don't tell them how to live," I said. I took his pencil from him and dropped it into his shirt pocket. Clasping his elbow, I turned him firmly toward the door.

"But—"

"No buts. Just go."

In minutes the ward was empty except for the new mother. She lay back on her bed in the center of the tight row of cots and settled her son next to her side. With her forefinger she stroked the wisp of black hair emerging from beneath his cap.

Later that day, Uncle gave me eight mandarin oranges left over from the special Tết dole. I accepted them because I didn't want to hurt his feelings, but felt uncomfortable eating the islanders' rations. What could I do with these nuggets of gold on an island of rice? I gave one to Monika, two to the shy daughter of the hospital cleaning woman, two to the mother of the New Year's baby with the yellow mittens, one to a child who'd climbed onto my lap during a hospital Tết party and one to her sister. That left the orange nibbled by a rat. I peeled it and, without letting on about the rat, shared its segments with the visiting journalist.

"Now we invite you to *xin xăm*—ask for a propitious future," a fresh-faced girl named Yêu said to me my third morning. Yêu was a member of the hospital clerical staff.

She had taken me to visit the pagoda, a bamboo structure overlooking the sea from atop Religious Hill. Afterward, she led me to a small altar outside the temple. There, paper lotus blossoms and bowls of green apples flanked a golden Buddha. Yêu, whose name meant "Love," instructed me to kneel and say my name.

"*Bà Mỹ!*" whispered a boy in a Saigon Army shirt. He pointed. Spectators jostled one another, pushing to see.

"Look! *Bà Mỹ*'s kneeling!" said a man wearing glasses.

I felt embarrassed and then angry at the gawkers. Struggling to hide these feelings, I told the Buddha my Vietnamese name, Lý. Spoken with a rising tone, it means "Plum Blossom" and "Reason."

"Make a wish," Yêu said, handing me a section of bamboo filled with long bamboo slivers.

"Now *Bà Mỹ* is making a wish," observed a woman wearing a freshly ironed blouse. She laughed, fluttering a fan of ration cardboard slip-stitched with pink hammock twine.

Irritated by this woman, I bowed, waiting for words to come. The crowd quieted; somewhere in the distance a child laughed. Silently, in Vietnamese, I asked the Buddha to help me contain my exasperation at Bidong's gawkers, who gathered like gnats around me wherever I went. Then I looked up and noticed that the Buddha was missing half of his right ear.

"Now shake it, Lý," Yêu said. Her soft voice was authoritative.

Bamboo rattled gently against bamboo.

"Oh no! Oh no, that won't do!" said an old woman carrying a toddler on each hip. She laughed. I saw she had no teeth.

"Harder!" the onlookers said.

"Shake the slivers harder!" said the woman in the neatly pressed blouse. She waved her fan at me and I felt its breeze brush back my hair. "Harder. Or your wish won't come true!"

That evening I sat with the journalist and Monika on the hospital balcony. Below, jetty lights illuminated the ribs of abandoned hulls that poked from the surf. These boats had once been fishing trawlers like *RC 2* before people leaving Vietnam purchased them to escape. Once the passengers had landed on Bidong, they stripped from the boats any usable materials—metal, deck and hull planking—for houses and furniture, leaving only the keels and ribs to the sea. The three of us watched the fragile light play over waves lapping around the wrecked boats.

"Too bad we can't magically clean up this island," the journalist muttered. He ran his forefinger along the scar cutting down his cheek.

Monika touched his arm. "You care too much, I think. It's enough to take little steps, isn't it? Like the small waves pushing in the tide."

"Perhaps," he said, looking at her.

"Perhaps, I think yes," Monika said, holding his gaze.

At 2 A.M., when we went to bed, the tide was high. The boat skeletons lay buried beneath the sea. The camp was quiet. The cooking fires no longer flickered and the snippets of twine clamped over kerosene had stopped sputtering. The last fragrance of incense in the Coconut Altar near the hospital drifted over the empty paths.

4
Any Day

Bidong was a community without cars, buses, bicycles, books, computers, photocopiers, calculators, typewriters, or telephones. On that island paper was rarer than gold. One crackly radio and several unpredictable boats connected it to the mainland three hours away. As an administrator, I didn't write memos, letters, feasibility studies, and project assessments in quadruplicate. Instead I ran errands. And I listened.

No day was typical, yet all were similar. Here is one day—it could have been any day—in my life on Bidong.

I awoke, stretched, and brushed rat droppings from my bed. Changing from a sarong into a shirt and Vietnamese peasant trousers, I splashed my face with water, tied up my hair, washed the previous day's clothes, and went outside to the toilet.

While buying bread in the black market for my breakfast, I patiently told the vendor that I was sorry but I couldn't order her special transfer to America. After breakfast, I arranged for the laboratory staff to work with a Malaysian health team investigating malaria, then placed an announcement on the loudspeakers for those with undiagnosed fever to come to the outpatient clinic. After asking Bach to find someone to clean out the storeroom to make a new TB examining office, I went to the baker's hut. Sweating next to his clay oven, I bargained smuggled flour confiscated by Malaysian guards in exchange for bread he would bake for the TB patients' extra rations.

As the baker and I were returning to the warehouse for the flour, I noticed that the loudspeakers were announcing the wrong time for the malaria screening. Annoyed, I stopped by the radio station to correct the announcement. When the station head asked if I could recover the speakers that were being repaired in Kuala Lumpur, I hurriedly (and reluctantly) added his request to my list of chores. In the sultry warehouse, I haggled about the brine-soaked sacks of flour with Uncle, who was being petulant.

Afterward, I took another visiting journalist on a quick tour of the island and chuckled to myself when he wanted to photograph the rats, which of course were nocturnal. He refused to stay overnight because of them. I told three United Nations staff about a baby who required immediate transport to the mainland hospital on the UN launch, stifling my exasperation at their extraneous questions because I badly needed their speedboat.

The malaria officials arrived and I showed them to the work space I'd arranged, then placed a reminder announcement at the radio station before chasing down an oxygen cylinder for the baby and making a note to radio the mainland for more. Next I found the father, who was to accompany the baby, told him when the boat would leave and explained Trengganu hospital-admission procedures. I located a mosquito net for a talkative man with leprosy. His numb toes were being eaten at night by the rats. On my way to the Malaysian guards' station to speed the baby's exit papers, I stopped by the new TB examining office and discovered the electrician had wired only one outlet instead of the two required. Irritated, I picked up the baby's exit papers and chased down the electrician.

I settled the baby onto the late afternoon launch. Just as the speedboat was beyond yelling distance, I noticed I was holding the medical report written to accompany the child. Furious with myself, I sprinted up Religious Hill to the radio and asked a staff person in the mainland office to transfer the report to the ambulance waiting for the child at the Trengganu jetty. For an hour I yelled the case history into the radio: "bloody and mucous stool, bloody, B-L-O-O-D-Y, mucous, M-U-C-O-U-S, stool, S-T-O-O-L, like you sit on." While shouting into the radio, I toyed with a bowl of *chè*, a sweet pudding made from dried peas, cautiously offered by the man who lived in the radio shack, then ran over to the pagoda to apologize for having completely missed my English class.

On my way back down Religious Hill, two strangers stopped me, requesting priority on TB screening X rays. I snapped at them and immediately felt guilty. After collecting a letter for a Bidong patient under treatment in mainland Trengganu, I checked on eighty-three new arrivals, among whom were twelve women and girls who'd been raped by Thai pirates. One girl was nine years old.

I ate supper, which that day was also lunch, and tried to ignore the MRCS social workers, who were squabbling again. For a few minutes I chatted with Flower, who wanted to know if it was really true that everyone in America drove a car. Then I taught intermediate English to seventy-five hospital workers, all of whom wanted to practice conversation but were afraid to talk. Thinking they might want to telephone a friend or relative as soon as they landed in the West, I described how to make a long-distance call. When their expressions remained puzzled despite several explanations in English and Vietnamese, I asked in both languages how many had used a phone. Only two of the seventy-five raised their hands.

After class I told two people whom I'd never seen before that I didn't have time to give private language lessons. Resentful and cranky by 10 P.M., I met with the deputy camp leader about a program of daily English classes to be played over the loudspeakers, then went to the shower and poured cold water over my head.

As I was returning from the shower, a young woman stopped me to request treatment for her baby, whose head was covered with purple carbuncles from infected mosquito bites. A stranger asked me to cash a personal check drawn on a bank in El Dorado, Arkansas; another stranger wanted me to assume full financial support for him, his wife, mother, and ten children after they arrived in the United States.

Flower was brushing her teeth when I passed the Coconut Inn. "Tomorrow we'll be out of firewood and short on rice," she said in Vietnamese, her mouth frothy with rationed toothpaste. She spat. Her duck nipped at the white foam.

"I'll talk to Uncle in the morning," I said wearily. "Get some rest now."

"*Ngủ ngon, nhé!*—Sleep sweetly, you hear!" she answered.

Just when I thought I could catch a few minutes of solitude, a man with a boy slung over his shoulder rushed into the emergency room. I called the surgeon, who ran tests. Within half an hour he and his assistant stood in green gowns, their scrubbed hands held up as if in prayer. A nurse shaved the boy's abdomen.

As the surgeon slit the skin, I thought of the cartoon with a chagrined Johnson hitching up his shirt to display a scar that bulged into the shape of Vietnam. The Bidong surgeon's incision was trim, less than two inches. Searching for the appendix, he pointed to worms squirming inside the boy's translucent intestines. Quickly he removed the appendix, completed the internal stitching, and sewed up the wound. The diseased organ, which was smaller than the tip of my little finger, lay on a surgical drape.

After the boy was settled, I returned to my room. Yeu brought me a plate of gelatin she'd made from black market eggs and seaweed. When she left, I tried to finish a letter I'd started before daybreak; suddenly homesick, I abandoned the letter in midsentence, sealing it. It was past 1 A.M. when I lay down. Two men who slept on the floor outside my room sang ever so gently,

Hò ho ho hó ho ho hò
Con ngủ ngủ đi con

Ho ho ho ho ho ho ho
Go to sleep my child.

I dozed off, but awakened abruptly to a rat scrabbling in the plate of seaweed gelatin.

My body reacted with continuing upheaval to Bidong. In New York I'd stepped from rib-snapping cold into an airplane and twenty-four hours later emerged, without layover, into temperatures close to a hundred. My biological clock had been knocked into its polar opposite so that I was sleepy by midmorning, yet wakeful after midnight. Suddenly I was living with thirteen thousand people in the same amount of space in which, before, I'd lived alone. I felt feverish, nauseated, and headachy. Much of the time I was tired and when I was discouraged, which was often, I counted the months until my departure in August, wishing for silence and someone to hold me.

The dietary change from vegetables and goat's milk to rice and black tea made me constipated, and although I drank and drank, I urinated at most once a day. For those six months my menstrual cycles stopped. But my sweat glands worked overtime. Perspiration slid down my arms and back and legs even if I stood in the shade of a palm tree. My hair remained damp during the day though it dried at night, stiffened by my own salt.

The morning heat exhausted me before my day began; by evening I felt as if I'd been oiled in sweat, rolled in sand, and deep-fat-fried. At 1 A.M. when I finally shut my door, I was so tired I couldn't sleep: as soon as I closed my eyes, I saw faces, a sea of them framed by bamboo and blue-striped plastic, and I heard voices and more voices, a hum rising and falling like the surf.

I felt as if I were two years old again. Learning a new language has that effect, and rejuvenating one dormant for years is no different. I heard sounds, but they rushed by in a frenzy like insects droning during a tropical night. I struggled to differentiate words, but caught nothing; and when I did try to speak, the listeners would stare blankly. Or worse, they'd laugh. Over and over, this trying cycle repeated itself until I wanted to scream with the ferocity of a toddler's tantrum.

Vietnamese is a difficult language for a Westerner because it's not spoken, but sung. In Western languages, tone communicates emotion or differentiates between a statement and a question; in Vietnamese, tone is the essence of each word.

Vietnamese is written in a modified Latin script introduced by a French priest in the eighteenth century. This alphabet has three "a's" and three "o's"; two "e's," "d's" and "u's"; and no "f," "j," "w" or "z." Diacritical marks written over or under a vowel indicate the word's tone. Any sequence of letters may have six possible tones; *each* of these tones signals a completely different word.

The two-letter configuration, *"la,"* for instance, is pronounced like the sixth note, "la," of the Western musical scale. However, tone differentiates that one configuration into six different sounds and meanings:

no tone	*la*—to shout
rising tone	*lá*—a leaf
falling tone	*là*—to be
low falling tone	*lả*—to be exhausted
high broken tone	*lã*—to be plain
low broken tone	*lạ*—to be strange

These six tones are hard for the Westerner to differentiate, and equally hard to duplicate. A Vietnamese listener who doesn't know a Western language won't understand the Westerner's obtuseness to tone, and therefore won't think to second-guess the gibberish or even vulgarity resulting from an incorrect choice. In Quảng Ngãi I never went into a shop to buy *phấn* (chalk), for example, without first consulting a dictionary because I feared pronouncing the wrong tone and offending the vendor by a request, instead, for a box of feces.

Unlike English, Vietnamese is consistent. Letters aren't pronounced in several ways as, for example, the "ou" in "cough," "tough," "through," "bough," and "dough." Vietnamese sounds have counterparts in English, including the "ng" as in "Quảng Ngãi" or "Nguyễn," the most common Vietnamese family name. This sound is pronounced much like the "ng" in "sing"; for Westerners the difficulty comes from its position at the beginning of the word.

Vietnamese grammar is easy for Westerners because it seldom uses tenses. Conversational context or the position of a time word takes the place of the many English tense variations. An auxiliary verb for present, past, or future may be added for clarity or emphasis, but this usage occurs relatively seldom.

At first, as I struggled to remember my Vietnamese, the speaker's words were only rushing sounds, but by the second or third time I'd heard a word, it slipped back into my listening vocabulary. Speaking vocabulary returned much more slowly.

I couldn't take ten steps anywhere on that island without someone stopping me. Since I was the only person among the MRCS, UN, or Malay Task Force guard staffs who spoke Vietnamese, I spun between the islanders and all those groups, constantly listening to requests that usually were impossible to grant.

English was also frustrating. Since others spoke it as a second language, I had to slow down like a record playing at the wrong speed while I chose the simplest words and pronounced them with the clearest possible enunciation.

From 6 A.M. straight through the glaring heat of the day until 2 A.M., I was besieged with words and more words, talk and more talk, a shock after years of solitude in an Appalachian valley where I could go for days without hearing the sound of another person. Then, at 2 A.M., the generator shuddered and stopped, and the silence was broken only by chattering insects and the restless breaking of the surf.

My life in Quảng Ngãi ten years before had had a slower pace, but behind it had been the war: the unnerving whine of mortars, the inescapable smell of decay. In 1969, the U.S. military rose to a half-million Americans—roughly one for every forty South Vietnamese citizens. American and Saigon troops patrolled Quảng Ngãi's outlying airstrip and two-lane road, but only by day. On late afternoons, the tanks rumbled back into the American compound as the town shrank into itself like a frightened mollusk.

Sometimes we spent nights in the bunker. There were ten of us on the Quaker team. Whatever spats we'd had at work crackled during supper and throughout the evening, sputtering in the bunker before they flared again the next day.

At meals I sat as far as possible from Joe, the limb maker. He was the crucial professional and he knew it. An Englishman in his late forties, he'd been a child during the bombing of Britain. Joe constantly bullied me except in the bunker, where he sat on the dirt floor, nervously chewing his pipe. The rest of us—Americans in our mid-twenties—leaned back against the dank sandbags and told stories. Outside, the darkness rattled and thumped.

One night in the bunker I sat next to Joe. That night the sky ripped. My eardrums shattered. The sandbags over my head shook, raining granules. I cringed in raw, lonely terror, my palms clenched against my ears while the darkness spewed fire. Joe grabbed my knees, sobbing as he ducked into my lap. Cowering, we held each other until long after quiet had returned and we had each lapsed into drowsiness.

The MRCS team on Bidong was constantly changing. When I arrived, the staff included a German doctor working with Monika in the tuberculosis screening program; Monika, the radiographer; Uncle and Selva, Malaysians of Indian origin who handled supplies; Kuan Ying, a Malaysian social worker of Chinese origin; Susan, a Malaysian social worker of Indian origin; Paul, a British engineer; Jim, an American who was general officer; and myself as health administrator.

We never needed staff meetings because we conducted business constantly during meals in the Coconut Inn. In Malay, Chinese, French, German, and English, we talked and bickered and pouted and stormed. And we laughed about the flies and the toilets and the rats.

When we went to the mainland, Jim and I shared an apartment, padding around it with platonic familiarity. He'd attended Jesuit schools in upstate New York before working with Catholic Relief Service in Nigeria and Sudan. Then he'd transferred to Lutheran World Service, which donated his time to MRCS for assignment to Bidong. On the island, the Vietnamese called him Big Jim because he towered over everyone in height and work.

Although he was in his early thirties, Jim looked forty-five. His gray hair was receding and his tobacco-stained teeth had a groove where he clamped his pipe. A paunch revealed his fondness for beer. He loved to swim, but when he did on Sunday afternoons, he dove off the jetty, driving himself with flippers down through depths that burst the capillaries in his nose, until he reached the bottom and checked the mooring anchors.

Of all the MRCS staff, I had the most contact with Monika. Early in the morning I'd hear Bach preludes on her tape recorder, then *Für Elise* late at night: she said that when she was home in Frankfurt, she liked nothing better than to play Bach's *Wohltemperierte Klavier*. Monika had worked as a laboratory technician in French-speaking Africa for seven years before coming to Bidong, her first experience of the Orient.

She loved the islanders. Hour after hour she locked herself inside the TB program's lead cubicle. Dripping sweat, growing thinner each day during her eleven months on Bidong, she shot ten thousand X rays, amusing me every time she described a Vietnamese as "You know, the one with the black hair." Yet she could remember hundreds of TB patients not only by the gray-on-gray image of their lungs but also by the correct pronunciation of their full names.

Monika and Jim's obsessive work frightened me, drawing me back into that destructively compulsive drive I'd felt when trying to write. With them I felt like a recovered alcoholic surrounded by soused drinking buddies. I never learned what drove them so; and they never learned what drove me.

Occasionally I joined Monika and the Vietnamese TB detection staff at one of the cafes on Zone C beach. By dusk, the market with its colorful stalls and tiered wares had vanished. In its place, people had set out rough tables and low benches they'd made from planks torn off ships wrecked on the sand.

One evening we picked a table near the waves. A tape recorder in one of the cafes carried a man's voice:

Ngưỡi nô lệ da vàng bước di bước di
Đi về đồi hoang/Đi . . .

Chained people of golden skin will strive and strive
Till they return to their abandoned hills
Till they speak with their brothers and sisters,
Reclaiming peace for their *quê hương*
Establishing a future for their ancestors.

For one ringgit (fifty cents in American money) a woman brought us coffee and sweetened condensed milk mixed to make a drink that tasted rich and thick like ice cream. As we sipped it, one of the Vietnamese men working with Monika spoke of waiting fifteen months to leave the island. At nineteen he had earned a reputation for delicate drawings with charcoal on ration cardboard. He talked of returning to Vietnam by way of the jungles of Kampuchea after he gained American citizenship. He would obliterate the Communists, he said. I shuddered as I imagined what would happen if thousands of aimless, unattached Bidong men like this one were to return to Vietnam, wearing khaki and carrying M-16s.

"Is enough of the fighting, don't you think?" Monika asked. Her eyes had a snap that no one argued with.

The man's voice softened. "More than anything," he said, "I want to return to my *quê hủổng*—my home, the location of my ancestors' graves." He gazed at the dark sea, which stretched on until it met a somber sky. "I'm just like every other Vietnamese, as rooted to my *quê hủổng* as a banyan tree."

All along the market beach, people sipped the rich, sweet coffee. "Must search for their *quê hủổng*/Must search for their *quê hủổng*/Must search for their *quê hủổng*" came the singer's refrain.

❂ 5

Fires in the Bottom
of a Well

One day a twelve-year-old girl fell into a well. Normally all wells on Bidong had fences, but since this particular one had gone dry, people sometimes removed the barricade to burn trash in the hole. The girl had been walking backward on a path, teasing another child, when suddenly she fell fifteen feet onto a bed of hot coals.

Neighbors heard the shrieks echoing upward from inside the black hole. A man tied a rope around his waist, and others lowered him down the side of the well into the darkness. When he reached the bottom, the man pulled the shrieking child from the coals and lifted her onto his hip. He signaled by jerking the rope, and the others pulled him and the child up inch by inch. Hands reached down, taking her from the man's arms and settling her onto a stretcher. Two men ran with the stretcher to the hospital, jostling the wailing, severely burned child.

As I entered the hospital, I heard her screaming. A bearded old man and a young woman with a baby rushed past me toward the intensive care room, where the child lay upon the stretcher. It was Sunday and no one had come to sweep the wards. Gauze squares yellow with pus littered the floors. Dust drifted through the open windows. Flies entered between the louvers that opened toward the main sewer. They lit on the yellowed gauze. In the intensive care room, they settled on the child's raw flesh, buzzing.

Nurses dabbed at her body with gauze, their fingers sometimes touching the wounds. The girl shrieked and squirmed and struck out with her good hand. Her cries attracted more onlookers from the beach. Spectators crowded into the intensive care room while the Vietnamese doctor-on-call chatted in the next ward. I chased the doctor in and the onlookers out, but the gawkers returned like flies.

The child's name was Thanh, which means "Serenity." Thanh shrieked until a nurse gave her morphine, and then it was half an hour before she quieted. We made a tent of sheets over her, but when I checked underneath, I recoiled in terror. Flies peppered the meaty expanse of Thanh's wounds. Her body was red and black and yellow all down the right side. She smelled of cinders and of burnt flesh. I insisted we send her and a relative as escort to the mainland on the next available boat.

Bidong was a Malaysian prison walled by the sea and guarded by wardens from a special Department of Prisons task force. Like the islanders, I had voluntarily entered that prison, but unlike the Vietnamese, I could always leave. Every few weeks I went to the mainland's central market to buy special rations for Bidong hospital patients, stopping at a vegetable stall run by a Chinese woman with rolls of fat under her chin. The first time I dealt with this vendor, I protested her doubled prices. She insisted in English. When a chicken I'd bought pecked one of her cucumbers, she ranted in Chinese and rearranged a pile of green mangos. Her arms and even her fingers were plump.

"The price stands," she said.

"I'll go elsewhere," I said, leaving. My flip-flops slapped against vegetables mashed on the market floor, throwing muck against my legs.

"For you! Only for you a special bargain!" The figures she called after me exceeded the usual ones.

"For your competitor, a big order!" I answered, reciting standard prices for three items.

"Okay. Okay-*la!*" she said. "But my children will starve and you'll see, I'll waste away to nothing."

"You'll see! You'll see!" a neighboring vendor called across her garlics. "Come tomorrow and she'll be thinner than a sprig of coriander."

My vendor laughed as she collected the order. She added carrots to the sack even though I hadn't requested them, and then an extra cabbage. She asked what had brought me to Trengganu and then asked question after question about Bidong.

After I'd loaded the groceries on a boat for Bidong, I went to the mainland hospital to see Quảng, a hepatitis case we'd transferred from the island. I sat on one side of his bed, and his wife sat on the other. The woman watched her husband with an expression of affection, her eyelids twitching. Her eyebrows arched as delicately as willow branches.

"I miss Bidong," Quảng said, waving toward the sea. His hand was the yellow of stagnant urine. "Can't we go back with you? I want to see my children."

I shook my head even though I knew Quảng might not last

much longer. "When you're discharged," I said, worried that
I was making the wrong decision.

"Then I'll stow away!" He laughed and rolled his eyes.

"The sweeties are warming up again," Jim said that evening in the Trengganu apartment. Every night the children
in the flat above the one we shared on the mainland would
run, squealing and thumping, the parents would yell and
then the children would wail until finally, hours later, there'd
be silence.

"You'd better come with us." Jim wore a beach towel
wrapped around his paunch as he shaved at the kitchen sink.
He was dressing to join Paul, the British engineer. They'd
been invited to dinner by a Kuala Lumpur contractor to
celebrate completion of the Bidong toilets. Listening to the
pounding feet above, I decided to take Jim's advice and go
along.

The contractor treated us to a Chinese feast with the full
twelve courses, including snail soup and fish eyes. Afterward
he insisted we take in the town's only disco. There, psyche-
delic lights flickered over the dance hall, which pulsed with
music heavy on snare drums and cymbals. In front of the
Malay musicians a Chinese singer swayed in a hip-slit dress,
its satin undulating over her hips.

A young woman sat down next to Jim as soon as the waiter
had shown us to a cluster of red velvet couches. She arranged
the slit of her dress to display a smooth brown thigh. Jim
puffed on his pipe. When she leaned toward him, stroking
the fine hairs on the back of his neck, he rose and settled into
an empty chair. She slid across the couch toward Paul. She
was Chinese and spoke no English; Paul was English and
spoke no Chinese, but they ushered each other onto the floor,
where they danced until midnight.

While the contractor moved from table to table, buying drinks, Jim and I sipped whiskey and nibbled small but intensely flavorful peanuts. In the apartment, even when Jim lounged with a beer, his mind would race on, exhausting me with more details to handle. In the disco, he leaned back against the red plush seat and watched the singer onstage.

"Let it be, let it be." The woman swaying at the microphone sang the Beatles' song with Chinese inflections. The musicians pressed toward the crescendo, "Whisper words of wisdom, Let it be."

Suddenly the lights snapped on. Dancers and drinkers rubbed their eyes. The rich velvet lounge chairs were dull and tired, with spills on the arms. The air smelled of whiskey; crushed peanut shells covered the floor. The room resounded with men's voices raised in slurred protest as a door at the far end of the dance hall closed behind the shimmering thighs of the young Chinese women.

While in Trengganu, I stopped by to see Thanh, the child who'd fallen down the well two weeks before. A green examining screen surrounded her bed. Cường, who was Thanh's boat leader, greeted me. Usually a family member accompanied each Bidong patient transferred to Trengganu. After we'd loaded Thanh onto *Red Crescent 2*, Cường had introduced himself as her cousin and her Head of Family's choice for escort because he spoke English. A small man in his mid-twenties, he wore glasses with one lens cracked.

Cường led me outside the ward where, like children, we peeped through flowered curtains at Thanh wrapped in white. She howled as nurses unwrapped the gauze, her cries piercing the air. Cường flinched. His knuckles whitened as he gripped the window bars. Thanh shrieked again.

Suddenly I'm back in Quảng Ngãi. A nurse from the burn ward stands near a child she's brought to soak in the Rehabilitation Center tub. The child, who's about ten, lies on a table. Her face has red spots that look like chicken pox; her legs are bandaged with gauze that is yellow and red and gray. She's been burned with napalm.

When the nurse starts to open a dressing on the girl's leg, the gauze begins to tremble. It assumes a life of its own. The smell of rotting flesh rises from the bandage. When the girl kicks and screams, I clamp her ankles; she twists against my grip. The nurse continues snipping. As she lifts the bandages, we both gasp.

The wound pulses with maggots squirming and wriggling in the rotting tissue. With a tongue depressor the nurse scrapes the larvae onto a gauze square. They wiggle, tumbling over one another. She digs for ones burrowing further into the fetid flesh. The child screams, and my throat clamps shut. I press my full strength against the child's ankles as maggots fall to the floor and lie there quivering. I step on them, feeling their bloated bodies pop and squish under my feet.

Listening to Thanh's cries, I tightened my grip on the window bars; I twisted the ball of my foot, grinding it into the earth.

Cường pulled his knuckles, cracking each one. Removing his glasses, he touched the corner of each eye with the tip of his little finger.

Later, Cường took me to see Quảng, the hepatitis patient. Since my visit the day before, Quảng hadn't eaten, passed urine, or responded to his wife's voice. When doctors tried to pull back the lids of his half-closed eyes, Quảng hit them; and when, at the doctors' request, Mrs. Quảng tried to feed her husband medicine, he bit her.

In the men's ward Quảng looked abandoned in his brown-striped hospital pajamas, his eyes half open and yellow, his face sallow. Cuổng snapped his fingers over Quảng's eyes, slapped his face, and pulled on his sideburns. Quảng only stared.

Despairing, Cuổng and I sat on opposite sides of Quảng's feet to wait for the doctors, who were making rounds. Mrs. Quảng stroked her husband's forehead. From two wards away, we could hear Thanh shrieking while the nurses changed her bandages.

"Can't they leave those bandages off?" Cuổng asked.

"No."

We traded English and Vietnamese vocabulary: "dust," "dirt," "flies," "bacteria," "infection," "gangrene."

"If they don't change Thanh daily," I said to Cuổng, "will you tell me?"

He nodded. "Tell me where you're from," he said.

"The United States."

"You work for the CIA, I think."

"Why do you say that?"

"Because you speak Vietnamese."

I laughed. I told Cuổng about working for the Quakers in Quảng Ngãi during the war, about my home in the Ohio hills and my house tucked into a cove of the valley farm.

"It must be sad living there all alone," he said.

I described the retarded children who rode my school bus, the ones who could talk and liked stories and the ones who talked incoherently and understood less. I told him about my neighbors and how each summer we stacked hay onto a wagon, climbed on top and rode to the barn, and how in late summer the goldenrod carpeted the hills in autumn yellow before the slopes broke into red and auburn and drifted toward brown. Cuống's eyes widened as I described how the snows came and how it felt to tumble down the meadow in an inner tube. I wrote out my address for him.

Cuống told me how he'd been arrested while stealing along the road to Huế after curfew. He drew a line down Quảng's leg as if a brown pajama stripe were the road and, pointing to Quảng's ankle, drew a semicircle for a checkpoint. The map of checkpoints he had made for himself had been inaccurate. He'd been imprisoned by the Communists for nine months.

After his release from prison, Cuống gave his gold to two friends who were collecting money to buy an engine and wood. Once the boat was finished, Cuống and ninety-four others gathered in sheds used for cows and pigs. One night, when the moon was only a sliver, they stole through the darkness to their boat. The sea was glassy during their trip, and they met no pirates. When they landed on a Trengganu beach, Cuống told his passengers to ignore the Malay onlookers who beat him.

"I knew the Malays had to flog me," he said, "to show their power."

He removed his glasses with their cracked lens and again touched the corners of his eyes. "Just before I left Vietnam," he said, "I knelt and kissed the earth."

We stood as the medical staff doing rounds approached. When one of the doctors tried to examine Quảng's eyes, Quảng winced and turned, pulling his knees to his chest. Cuống leaned on Quảng's rib cage, and the doctor pried open the eyelid. The white of the eye was yellow. The doctors moved on.

The head nurse brought an IV drip. Cuống pressed against Quảng's shoulders, another nurse secured his forearm and I held his fist. The head nurse slipped the needle into Quảng's arm, but he jerked and it poked through the vein, causing it to bleed. Other nurses came, and we switched places so that the nurses stood on either side of Quảng; Cường and Mrs. Quảng stood at her husband's head and I at his feet. Eight of us pressed against Quảng while the head nurse concentrated. When she jabbed, he jerked, and once more the vein slipped away.

"Talk to him," the head nurse said.

"But he doesn't hear anything," Cường answered.

"Sometimes they hear," I said.

The nurse chose a vein and swabbed the skin. When she looked up, we leaned into Quảng. Against his yellow limbs our knuckles stood out, white.

"Don't move, brother Quảng! Don't move!" Cường yelled.

Quảng didn't listen. He jerked, yet the needle held. Quickly the head nurse taped it to his forearm while another nurse splinted the arm and tied it to the bed railing. Then the nurses moved quietly on, leaving Quảng strewn out on the cot. Quảng's wife stroked his hair as she looked down into his yellow eyes. Her eyelids twitched. Tears rolled down her cheeks and dropped onto her husband's face. He stared blankly back.

On Bidong, several days later, there was a knock at my door before daybreak. The young Vietnamese man who lived in the radio shack atop Religious Hill had come to fetch me.

"Message for you, Miss Lý," he said.

I changed from my sarong into Vietnamese trousers and, tying up my hair, gathered my pencil, notes, knife, and scissors, dropping them into my pockets.

Atop Religious Hill, the radio crackled. "Bidong to Control," I called. "Bidong to Control. Over." "Control" stood for the Trengganu MRCS office.

"That you, Lý?" Wan Jafoor, a Malay who handled arrivals and departures to and from Bidong, never used the prescribed radio jargon.

"Why so blooming early, Wan?" I shouted into the microphone.

"It's Quảng." Wan's voice shook over the static. "He's dead. Wife admitted to hospital. Collapsed with grief."

"You okay, Wan?" I yelled back.

"Sort of. What do I do with Quảng?"

"Bury him."

"But she wants to send him to the island."

"Can't, Wan. Just can't." I glanced apprehensively at the graveyard ridge, where the sun was beginning to rise, brazen with heat. I looked out over the sea that stretched on and on and remembered how quickly in the tropics a body will begin to bloat and then to seep.

"Too far, Wan. Too hot. Have to bury him on the mainland. Get Cường to help. The man with the cracked glasses. Tending the burned girl. Speaks good English. Name's Cường. C-U-O-N-G. Cường. Over."

"Okay-la. Thought you'd want to know."

I left the radio hut, only nodding to the young man who'd fetched me. As I walked down Religious Hill, I could feel tears coming. Slipping my hands into my pockets, I felt for my penknife and pencil. Slowly I ran my fingers along the curved grip of my scissors. Quảng had asked to come home; now I couldn't forgive myself for having denied his request.

❧ 6
Comings and Goings

On Bidong there were always boats: boats to be met, boats to be unloaded, boats to be sent off. Daily, *Red Crescent 2* arrived with pack rations, generator parts, drugs, or rolls of blue-striped plastic. Perhaps six times in as many months, the little vessel with its scarred hull brought cabbages. Once there was chicken, and the ripe smell of fowl hung over the camp. Cleavers whacked as boat captains doled out the meat. Two men scuffled over a carcass; one hacked the other's forearm to the bone.

Every two days, the tug hauled a huge, squat barge from the mainland to Bidong's intake pipe leading to the fresh-water tanks; every three days, the dumpy tug labored out to sea with the ponderous weight of the rubbish barge. At regular intervals, the UN launch sped in with delegations, journalists and resettlement officers; every day or so *Black Gold*, a World War II landing craft, lumbered away with departees.

Often there were unscheduled arrivals, such as the time a Malaysian fishing trawler appeared towing a refugee boat.

Vietnamese crowded the decks of the trawler, squatting on the hatches and clutching the cabin. More huddled in the towed vessel's bilge; a boy clung to its ribs, his feet slipping into black water that smelled of petrol and vomit. Empty fresh-water containers floated around his feet, jostling against a little girl with curly hair.

A longshoreman lifted the girl from the bilge. After she collapsed on her way down the jetty, he carried her to the hospital. The first-aid team brought in more people on stretchers. And more still.

In the hospital, I propped the curly-haired child, who was perhaps ten, against the crook of my arm and fed her sips of water. Her eyes were like dull sheet metal; they seemed to notice nothing. When I spoke to her, she barely murmured, and when I removed her blouse, which was dripping with rancid water, her arms sank like a rag doll's. The palms of her hands were wrinkled like slices of dried apple.

The next morning I looked into the children's ward and saw the little girl washing her hair over a tin basin. A Buddhist nun poured a thin, steady stream of water onto the back of her head. In the kitchen that afternoon I noticed the child lifting her tin bowl to the kettle steaming with *cháo*—rice soup. Two days after that, when I inquired about her, the nun said she'd left the hospital. I looked wistfully through the louvered windows at throngs of people on the camp paths, remembering the softness of the child's curls against my wrist. I never saw her again.

Sometimes the newcomers rammed their small boats directly up onto the beach; sometimes they landed on the mainland, and MRCS brought them out on *Red Crescent 2* or *Black Gold.* Occasionally a supply ship serving one of the offshore oil rigs would rescue a sinking boat.

Even though independent shipping companies owned the supply boats, oil executives forbade the captains to rescue Vietnamese. One captain, a wiry Dutchman, told me the oil executives had directed him to turn his fire hoses on any drowning boat people who tried to scramble aboard his ship.

Yet by late spring of 1980, hardly a day passed without an oil ship chugging up alongside the landing barge, a row of dark heads and gold faces peering down over the ship's railing. For several weeks, one particular vessel arrived every three or four days. One day this ship's captain radioed that he carried seventy-seven on board.

Since the tide was low, he anchored offshore. I rode out on the Malaysian guards' outboard. As we approached, I could see the captain surrounded by Vietnamese children eating sandwiches. He was a burly man, bald, with a magnificent gray beard streaked in gold. He wore shorts and no shirt and was deeply tanned. Children stroked the thick hair covering his legs, arms and chest. The captain moved away from them when I stepped on board.

"You must be a Quaker," he said, stretching out his hand. His grasp was muscular.

I was taken aback. "Well, not card-carrying," I answered. I'd never joined a Quaker meeting.

"Then meet another independent," he said, laughing. The captain, I found out later, came from an old Philadelphia family with a name I recognized as Quaker. This was his last trip to Bidong before he went on home leave to a yacht he moored in the Mediterranean.

"How much water off that jetty?" he asked, scanning the mud flats strewn with boat skeletons.

"Twenty feet. What do you draw?"

"We'll make it." He gave orders to the first mate.

"Any sick ones?" I asked.

"Not after we gave them water."

As the ship eased toward the pier, the captain ushered me into the galley. "Would you like some ice cream?" he asked after we'd settled into a booth.

"Ice cream!" I couldn't think of anything to offer in exchange for such a luxury. Then I remembered how I'd felt on *Erma* after we'd spent days on the water. "Would you like to come ashore?" I answered.

The ship's cook served freshly brewed coffee with real cream. He removed bowls from a cabinet and opened the freezer.

"What made you think I was a Quaker?" I asked as I savored the coffee.

"You're a woman and you're here."

We'd just finished our ice cream when the engineer shifted into reverse. The boat shook. The captain and I left the cabin and stood on the foredeck, watching the Vietnamese passengers mass along the rail; they hung over it as they called to islanders on the mooring barge.

"How long before I leave for America?" asked a man in a soiled T-shirt.

"Is Nguyễn Dục Thiep on your boat?" a longshoreman yelled back.

"How many of you?" called a member of the receiving team, jamming batteries into his megaphone.

"Look! How beautiful!" A woman pointed toward the blue houses nestled beneath the green sweep of palms.

"Seventy-seven," said a man with one arm. "Three boats. Ours picked up two others. Then we started to sink."

"Pirates?" asked the man with the megaphone as he switched on the power.

"Has DN 6013 arrived?" asked a passenger, touching on

his lapel the tiny square of black cloth that signified mourning. "It left three days before us."

"*Ngồi xuống! Ngồi xuống!*—Sit! Sit!" the megaphone rasped.

"Three pirate attacks," a man answered. The woman next to him began to weep. Bruises covered her jaw.

The Vietnamese receiving team boarded the ship and counted the new arrivals, who squatted in rows on the deck. "All right!" the megaphone called. "Ill and elderly off first. Women carrying babies second."

Standing together, the captain and I watched the new arrivals climb one by one over the ship's bulwark and file down the jetty. As soon as they had left, the crew turned the fire hoses onto the deck, blasting crusts of bread into the sea. When all was shipshape, the captain falsified his log and stepped ashore for lunch in the Coconut Inn. After six weeks on open water, he and his crew swayed down the jetty like ships in a high sea.

"Mr. Captain!" An old woman wearing a blouse with a mandarin collar called out. Age spots covered her face and hands. She ran up and, taking the captain's hands in hers, snuffled his hairy forearms, covering them with oriental kisses. "This one, he's the one," she announced to neighbors in the surrounding shanties. "Pulled us from the sea, this one did!"

A man wearing a pressed white shirt approached. He stopped and stared at the captain. "Yes," he said in English as he came forward. He bowed from the waist and extended his hand. "You save my boat. How I thank you." Before the captain could reply, the crowd pushed him on.

"New arrivals!" the loudspeakers screeched, giving the license numbers of the three boats and the number of passengers in each. "And on the island is the oil captain who's rescued the most boats."

Children surged around the captain. One of his crew, a lanky Swede, lifted two little boys onto his shoulders. Other boys grabbed his elbows, pleading to be next. When we reached the Coconut Inn, the captain and his crew stepped inside; the children hung over the half wall, crowding and pushing.

"Look!" said one boy wearing no shirt. "He's drinking tea."

"Incredible!" said another. "The one who drives the big ship has fur on his arms!"

Flower served the men sweet-and-sour soup. She sent her assistant to the black market for squid, which she sautéed in fish sauce and garnished with coriander grown in Zone F. For dessert she cut up a green mango she'd picked near the Coconut Inn. Smiling, she dipped a sliver into salt and offered it to the captain.

"Well, this beats ice cream," he said, stroking the streaks of gold in his beard.

Later, after more tea, the captain and his crew left the Coconut Inn for their ship. The camp followed, buoying them the way the sea carries off flotsam from a wrecked boat.

No one knows how many boat people never made it. The Vietnamese said more drowned than landed. Some Malaysians stopped eating fish; they said it tasted of decay.

Once, when I was running up Religious Hill to the radio, I stopped abruptly, my breath taken away. There, before me, stood a life-sized sculpture of an old man pulling a young woman from waves that had consumed all but the bow of their boat. Made of orange clay dug from the mountainside, the sculpture glistened with wetness. The artist stood nearby with knife in hand as he appraised his work. He added lines around the old man's eyes, accenting his haggard look, then wrote "VN" on his frail beard, which curled into the shape of Vietnam.

A few days later, I noticed cracks searing the clay face of the young woman. Some days after that, the old man's hands split and fell away.

One night as I left supper in the Coconut Inn, a little boy took my hand. He stroked the hollow of my palm and looked up at me expectantly. The top of his head came to my waist. His hair fell in a neatly clipped line across his forehead, and unusually long lashes shielded his eyes. He tugged on my hand.

"Where are we going?" I asked in Vietnamese.

"For a walk."

He led me toward the beach, where the sand was soft and still warm underfoot. It was dusk, the time when the sea drew everyone to her. People squatted in the sand and sat all along the jetty, dangling their feet over the edge. Toddlers squealed as they dragged ration-tin boats through the foaming surf.

The child led me up Religious Hill, past the Catholic church and the pagoda to a steep path. We scrambled down between houses perched on the cliff. Soon we were on Zone C beach, where islanders sat at the low tables, sipping thick, sweet coffee.

From there the boy led the way back into the camp. We passed stalls lit by single kerosene wicks that threw wavering light on displays of cigarettes, New Zealand apples and hard candies. From a bakery hut came the smell of hot, fresh bread. In the Coconut Inn the cooks were playing Chinese Friends, a game resembling chess. Farther down the path, adults in a shed studied English by kerosene light.

Finally, the boy led me into a neighborhood with a maze of paths so narrow that my shoulders brushed against gunny-sacks and cardboard. Every time someone approached us, the child stopped and turned sideways, holding my hand tighter. We stepped over ditches filled with cans, plastic ra-tion bags, and garbage. The path twisted so often that I lost my bearings until now and then I'd hear the sound of the sea. Then we ducked around the trunk of a palm tree and, sud-denly, stepped into a house. As I entered, the boy's mother laughed nervously. Her son laughed too, covering his mouth with his hand.

The hut was the size of my room in the camp hospital. The light of a kerosene wick flickered off walls made of ration boxes spread out one over the other. The cardboard was stamped with the MRCS crescent moon in red and the UNHCR world map in blue. The plastic roof had holes in it. In the corner of the hut, coals smoldered in a fire pit made of packed earth. With chopsticks a young woman clipped the embers and deposited them in a milk tin she held between pieces of ration carton cardboard. Replacing the lid, she shook the container and then, rolling it, ironed a shirt.

"Welcome, Miss," said a man with long, thin fingers. He lifted a bamboo flute to his lips and blew a delicate trill.

"A sugar-cane bird lives here," said the mother of the little boy who'd led me to the house. She laughed with a high-pitched, nervous tone and invited me to sit on the hut's bamboo bed. Above it, a baby slept in a tiny hammock that swayed as a girl pulled on twine tied to it.

The family gathered around. Neighbors crowded into the room, blocking the doorway; the air grew so close that my shirt stuck to my back. A plump woman fanned me with ration cardboard as the little boy sat between his mother and me, his arm sticky against mine. He lifted a wisp of my cinnamon-colored hair and laughed out loud when it sprang back, coiling around itself. His mother removed an instant-coffee jar from the hut's only shelf and poured water, which she offered. The water had a brackish taste. We began to talk.

In Vietnam, I used to call such conversations "twenty questions." On Sundays in Quảng Ngãi when I'd walk alone around the town, people often invited me into their homes. "How old are you?" they'd ask. "How many children do you have?" "Are your parents living?" "Do you have brothers and sisters?" "How much money do you make?"

"How old are you?" the woman fanning me began.

"Shhhh!" my little friend's mother replied. "The loud-speakers said never to ask Americans their age." Then she switched to Chinese and raised her voice. The sounds rattled in her throat.

Overhead, palm fronds scratched the plastic roof. Loud-speakers tied in the trees squawked with an English lesson. "How long have you been in America?" a woman read in a singsong voice.

"It's all right to ask." I spoke in Vietnamese to the boy's mother. "I'm thirty-seven to Americans, thirty-eight to you," I said, alluding to the custom of adding a year at Tet instead of on the actual birthday.

"Me too!" she said, smiling a lopsided grin. "We're both born in the Year of the Horse."

"Ah, a horse," onlookers crammed into the doorway said to one another, nodding.

"I have been in America two months," a man on the loud-speakers announced.

"Have you brothers and sisters?" the flute player inquired.

"Month," the broadcaster repeated. His voice was definitive. "Day. Week. Month. Year. I have been in America two months. I have been in America two years."

"Yes, two brothers," I said.

"I have three sisters and four brothers," the woman on the loudspeakers said, giving each syllable the same emphasis. "I-am-the-eld-est."

"Do you have children?" my little friend's mother asked.

"Yes."

"How many?"

"Oh, on Bidong, maybe two thousand."

The little boy leaned his cheek against his mother's shoulder. He laughed, and his eyes disappeared behind his curling lashes.

"And your trip?" I asked.

"*A!*" the mother muttered. "Two hundred and ninety-five of us in a space like six huts." Glancing around the densely packed shanty, I could feel sweat slide down my back. "Two days without food and water," she continued. "Water was all we could think of." She refilled my jar. "The Vietnamese Communists are cruel. They give only three kilos of rice per person per month when an adult needs twenty-one. There's no gas for motorcycles nor batteries for radios. And there are no jobs to make money to buy anything."

I nodded, knowing that there in the crowded hut on Bidong I'd never be able to explain how American dollars had created a market among Vietnamese for Western consumer goods unavailable before the war and unaffordable after.

I remembered passing a Quảng Ngãi cafe in early 1969 just after its owner had hooked up a television. South Vietnamese soldiers jostled for a glimpse of the screen. Street boys peered through the window the way we kids had when an elderly bachelor bought our neighborhood's first TV.

By the time I left Quảng Ngãi in 1971, television aerials rose above the stucco shops. Several storekeepers had purchased the town's first cars. By 1971 American tanks had destroyed the paddy dikes; the province depended on rice imported from Louisiana until 1975, when the war ended and the United States terminated all shipments of consumer goods and food. Now there was no choice for the 53 million people who remained in Vietnam but the toil of rebuilding.

"Soon maybe we'll go to Cali," the mother said in a low voice, referring to California, where many islanders hoped to settle.

Her son took my hand when I rose to leave. He led me back into the maze of paths that twisted between cardboard houses. In front of the hospital he let go of my hand.

"This is where you live," he said.

"Good night," I said. "Come and see me again."

He folded his arms across his chest and bowed, stepping slowly back into the shadows.

Every morning the boy who'd taken me to his mother stood behind the Coconut Inn's half wall and watched me eat breakfast. Monika called him my shadow. "Lý! Lý!" the boy would call as soon as I finished my tea. I'd take his hand and together we'd walk to the hospital. Later, whenever I left the hospital to run an errand, Shadow would be there at the entrance, where he caught my hand in his.

One morning perhaps a month after my visit to his house, Shadow was absent from the Coconut Inn. As I finished my last bite of bread, his mother passed the asbestos half wall. She carried a bulging gunnysack on her shoulder.

"We're on the movement list!" she called, smiling with her lopsided grin. I knew 180 islanders were leaving that day for Kuala Lumpur, where they would stay until their exit papers cleared.

"I'll see you at the jetty!" I answered. Suddenly the loss

struck me. I was remembering the glass of water she'd offered as her family began its twenty questions. I remembered the feel of Shadow's small, moist hand in mine.

The departees had boarded *Black Gold* by the time I reached the jetty. I hurried on board, but since I didn't know Shadow's name—I'd always called him "Little Brother"—I could only watch for him. Children in puffy orange life jackets swarmed like bumblebees over the decks, their flip-flops making a *whisk-whisk* sound as sticky rubber lifted from the burning metal. All the children had straight black hair; all had black eyes with curling lashes.

I recrossed the deck, standing on tiptoe to search. The ship's horn blew twice and the boatmen cast off as I circled. Then the horn wailed one sustained note. As the stacks belched smoke, I dashed up the stairs to the gunwale. There I froze. The longshoremen had removed the loading ramp; below me, the sea churned into white froth. Catching my breath, I leaped across the widening span, my rubber sandals landing upon the edge of the mooring barge.

Black Gold's engines revved, and for a moment their roar overpowered the farewell shouts. As the people on the boat waved from behind the ship's bulwark, I berated myself for having left the Coconut Inn too late.

Then suddenly Shadow was leaning over the bulwark. "Lý! Lý!" he called, reaching out with his hand. I laughed with joy. We stretched toward each other and touched fingertips as the sea between us foamed and *Black Gold* pulled away.

There were always farewell parties on Bidong. One evening, Bảo, a doctor, led Monika and me through the center of the camp to his good-bye celebration. Bảo's wife had escaped by a different route to France, and now he was joining her. Effectively single in a culture that centered on family, he'd devoted time left over from the outpatient clinic to helping Monika with the TB program.

The house we visited in Zone B belonged to two brothers. Spacious by Bidong standards, it had a board bed made of deck planks and above the bed a hammock woven from the pink plastic twine Uncle issued. Bảo's friend boiled water over a fire pit. He served tea in instant coffee jars and passed around bowls of *chè*, the perennial pudding made from cooked peas mashed with sugar. When I'd first eaten *chè* in Quảng Ngãi, I'd gagged at its pasty consistency, but I'd long since come to relish it.

"We'll never again know each other as well as tonight," Bảo said to us regretfully.

"If ever we are wealthy," Monika said, "we have only to travel the world and visit our friends."

We took turns singing. Without radio and television, everyone on Bidong became a poet and performer. Bảo turned through a children's exercise book into which he'd copied his favorite verses. Throughout each song his voice was clear and plaintive, trembling like a violin around each note.

"Is there a Vietnamese song that doesn't sound sad?" Monika asked.

"Maybe for children," Bảo answered.

Bảo's friends asked me to sing in Vietnamese.

"Kẻ thù ta đâu có phải là người.—Our enemy is not people," I started.

"Giết người đi, thì ta ở với ai?—If we kill each other, whom shall we live with?" Bảo finished.

I said I didn't know the rest.

"Neither do I," Bảo answered. When he asked for a funny song in English, I sang, "There was an old lady who swallowed a fly/I don't know why she swallowed the fly/Perhaps she'll die."

"NHEEEEEAAA—" The loudspeakers directly overhead screeched.

Monika covered her ears. "The Section of Noise is at it again! Why don't you chew the speaker wires?" she added, kicking at a rat that flitted around her feet.

When the screeching subsided, she looked around and laughed. "Optimists are people who live beneath loudspeakers and still sing."

7
A Journey

Dr. Nguyễn Gia Thọ was the greatest optimist on Bidong. At first he seemed too easygoing to me, the way he was always slipping from one group to another, talking and laughing, covering his toothy smile with thin fingers. I knew he'd been a major with the Saigon Air Force and although he'd never given me reason to think this, I assumed he was a militarist. Thus I felt apprehensive when the Vietnamese doctors made him Assistant Head of Health. Now I could no longer avoid him.

One night Thọ asked if I wanted to see what he called his "piloting manual." He removed from his shirt pocket a small notebook with pages covered in fine, crosshatched lines peculiar to pads made in Vietnam. On the first page he'd listed rules for navigating a journey.

"But you've written this in English," I said, looking up in surprise.

"Yes," he answered, laughing. "For benefit of Communist police, who cannot read English."

I turned the page and found that he'd filled the rest of the book with diagrams, trigonometric tables, and data on the stars, the tides, and the currents. He'd listed the coordinates for all Southeast Asian refugee camps from the Philippines south along Thailand and Malaysia to Indonesia.

"Also, I use my head," Tho said, taking the small book when I handed it back to him. "In Vietnam, so we can go, I obtained false Chinese papers."

"Why Chinese?"

"Because the Vietnamese Government was letting out large numbers of ethnic Chinese. The government feared them since the Chinese invasion in 1978. I studied Cantonese for six months in order to defend my papers in case police stopped me. Then I bought a boat and sold vegetables."

"Cabbages?" I asked, teasing.

"Lots of cabbages. I went up river, bought vegetables from the farmers and sold them downriver in Saigon. Back and forth I went. My skin grew dark like fishermen's. Everyone knew me because my boat went up and down the river.

"One night I loaded the deck with vegetables. Below the deck I hid my wife, our seven children, and our six brothers and sisters. I told them, 'Be quiet, now. No one talk.' I piloted my boat down the river, and I waved to everyone.

"I intended to go to Indonesia but the wind—the monsoon that time is southwest—and the currents driven by wind did not allow. So I headed for Malaysia, to Kuala Trengganu. But the currents in the Gulf of Thailand drove me near Songkhla. I asked my wife if she wanted to land at Thailand. She refused. So we sailed along the west coast of the Gulf of Thailand. We met pirates, the Thai boats, southeast of Songkhla."

He touched the shirt pocket that held his small notebook, pausing. From the beach below came the plaintive trill of a bamboo flute. "I consulted my piloting manual and chose

Pulau Bidong. After four days at sea, I slept three hours. Then we went on. Finally, I piloted around Religious Hill and saw a crowd on the beach. Everyone cheered when we landed.

"When we arrived on Bidong, I felt jubilant. Now I understand that Vietnamese like me must scatter over the earth. Our country is lost to us. This island is our last Vietnam."

While we were on Bidong, Thọ and I bantered about who would leave the island first for Ohio. His sponsor, a doctor who'd been with the U.S. Army in Danang, lived in Cincinnati. It was there Thọ planned to settle his family. As it turned out, I left one day before Thọ. After my return from Malaysia, I visited him at the farmhouse he'd rented in the midst of a modern development.

"My home is another Bidong," he said one evening a year after he'd arrived in Ohio. We sat drinking wine with his wife and brother-in-law in their kitchen. A dozen children from four families played in the next room. In one year, Thọ and his wife had assumed full financial support for their seven children and twenty-six additional boat people.

"I've changed my goals," Thọ said, as he told me he'd developed diabetes. Now he assumed his life span would be shortened. I winced at this news. Thọ's name meant "Longevity," and I'd come to regard him as invincible.

"Still," he said, glancing at his wife, "she doesn't want me to, but some day I hope to join my fellow countrymen. They train to enter the jungles of Kampuchea, to overthrow the Vietnamese Communists. Perhaps you have read about this?"

"Yes," I said. "I know."

"But the first priority is the security of my family. My children are young, and maybe I won't live to be old."

Thọ told me how hard he'd studied for the medical

equivalency exams he'd just passed. He grew animated as he talked about his work at the University of Cincinnati Medical School. For two years laboratory technicians there had struggled to keep epithelial colon cells alive. After one month Thọ had broken through to a method. Now he was studying the cells' response to microorganisms in order to isolate the germs responsible for infection following abdominal surgery. His findings were to be published in a medical journal and presented at a conference in Boston.

"How did you figure that out, about keeping the colon cells alive?" I asked.

Thọ covered his toothy smile. "I studied the problem."

I laughed, for whenever I'd presented him with an apparently insurmountable difficulty on Bidong, he'd said, "I will study the problem. Tomorrow we will talk."

"For the colon cells," he continued, "I think like a Vietnamese. You know manioc? It is good for the digestion." I nodded, remembering the fibrous tuber I'd eaten in Quảng Ngãi. "I think about manioc, and that gave me the idea to try the sugar, mannose. It worked!"

That visit, I asked Thọ if I could see his piloting manual once again and if I might copy his rules for undertaking a journey. These I later tacked onto the wall next to my desk:

1. Always remember to carry a mirror.
2. Protect the watch and wind it regularly.
3. Keep out of the direct rays of the sun.
4. Keep a sharp look out at all times and do not pass up any chance of rescue.
5. Work as a team and make the wisest use of all information and aids available.
6. Use the most accurate methods available.
7. Establish a regular routine and keep busy.

8. Navigate with whatever means are available. Do not guess if there is any way of making a measurement or estimate.
9. Establish a democratic method of government, but when a leader has been chosen, cooperate fully with him. If he is competent, trust his judgment.
10. Maintain good morale. Do not permit conversation to become pessimistic. Good leadership qualities.

That same visit I'd brought copies of several music tapes I'd recorded on the island. Just before I left the next morning, Thọ presented me with a cassette containing the story of his family's trip across the South China Sea to Bidong. It was spoken by his nine-year-old daughter, Thủ-Trung, to her third-grade class in Goshen, Ohio. The accompanying typescript had pronunciation notes in Thọ's hand. Knowing his poetic ability in English as well as in Vietnamese, I suspect the script was one that father and daughter had worked on together, sharing its creation as they had shared their journey.

My name is Thủ-Trung Nguyễn. I was born on May 25th, 1972, in Vietnam.

I left my country on January 23rd, 1980 with my parents, my brothers and sisters, my uncles and aunts on a small wooden boat, 10 yards long, and 2 yards wide. My father was a physician and a major in the Vietnamese Air Force of the Republic of Vietnam. He was prisoner of the Communists within 3 years. Because of his scientific career, he was liberated from the jungle prison. But his life was unsafe and he feared all the time, after he had got out of the prison under the restricted control of the Communists, so he bought a small boat, he mounted a small engine of 7 horse-powers in it. And he brought my whole family to the small boat, came down along the Saigon River, watching everyone suspected around, escaping from our fatherland. We left the riverside at 6:00 PM and came to the sea at 11:00 PM. The waves were very rough. The wind blew at level 6. Night was very dark. The small boat rolled up and down on the sea. All of my brothers and sisters, my uncles and aunts, and I were sea-sick and continued vomiting. Except my mother who was holding a small kerosene lamp near the small, round and old helicopter compass for my father could see it to pilot the boat. At 6:00 AM the next day, our boat was very far from the South-East of the Vietnamese seashore. The open sea was very immense and deeply blue. The waves were very high and large. At first my father wanted to land at Indonesia but the wind and the waves were not suitable, so he piloted the boat at 240 degrees to Malaysia. Really he did not want to land at Malaysia because we had to pass across the gulf of Thailand where there have been a lot of sea pirates.

The next night, the sky was suddenly darkened. Some dark clouds suddenly appeared in cumulus. The wind suddenly blew from all directions. The fear appeared on my father's face. Storm was coming. He used the battery to light the car beam light mounted in front top of the boat to see clearly the waves coming ahead. Suddenly, the stern was lifted off from the water surface and the boat rotated, did not run as well. My father seriously looked at the bow to find out the direction of the waves coming. The beam light worked well, but it was too tiny with the deep darkness around. We prayed. My mother collected everything floatable for the rescue purposes. We feared. A lot of things inside the boat rolled over from side to side. Even all of us also wanted to be rolled over. My father carefully and seriously avoided each rage wave coming. And when he saw some stars appearing through a hole of the thick clouds in the sky, he cried: "Thanks God, we are surviving. We are still alive." Late in the second night, we saw the lighthouses of the Hon Khoai island, the far west island of Vietnam. And that means we were leaving the last part of our fatherland seashore. The third day, we began to come into the gulf of Thailand. The sea surface was smooth. We enjoyed opening the side windows to watch fishes swimming. A lot of sharks were following our small boat. Some sharks were swimming across underneath our boat. They were enjoying our boat or they were waiting for us as their preys, I really did not know. Our boat was very small and weak to win the sea current of the gulf, so she crossed it in zigzag with the flow of the tides. It took the whole that day and night to come nearby the west side of the gulf.

But unluckily, in the early morning of the 4th day, we met the sea pirates. They used weapons to rob. They disordered everything in the boat to look for gold and dollars, even the clothes we were wearing. They threw all our personal papers to the sea. They threw everything not valuable to the sea. Our parents prayed to them in the manner of the Buddhists. We feared and cried out. They cut off the rudder cable. Then they left. And we lost our last penny. But still luckily, they did not take the compass, and the engine was still in good condition. Food, water and oil were still enough. We still cried out when the pirates left far away. But my father was very brave. He wiped off our tears. He wiped off my mother's tears. Then he said solemnly: "Forget it. Children, arrange everything in order. We continue our way." Water filled up until the half of the boat. We used the empty oil cans to pour water out of the boat. My father repaired the cable of the rudder. We started the engine and piloted the boat southwards, along the West coast of the gulf of Thailand.

That night, we went through a float of thousands of fishing

boats of Thailand. My father turned off the small kerosene lamp in the cabin. We closed all the windows of the boat. My father reduced the engine power and our boat filtered through them safely, after almost 6 hours of fearing of being robbed again. My father was very tired. 4 nights of no sleep. He told us that we were at the sea border of Malaysia and Thailand. He anchored the boat near Kota Baru and took a sleep when my older brothers and sisters, my uncles and aunts were watching guardians turn by turn.

In the early morning of the fifth day, the 28th of January, 1980, our boat directed to Kuala Trengganu. My father looked healthy again after some hours of sleep. The happiness appeared on his face. He felt that every danger had passed. Leave the doctrine of Communism. Leave the Thai pirates. The sea was beautiful. The ranges of mountains of the West Malaysia were beautiful. The Malaysian fishing boats were fishing quietly, laboriously and lovely.

At 4:00 PM of the same day, we landed at Pulau Bidong, an island belonging to Kuala Trengganu State of West Malaysia, one border of the free world at the South-East of Asia.

8
The Flamingo

"I understand their feeling, what is like to walk down that pier onto Bidong Island," said Dr. Cung, the camp leader. He and I were standing together beside the window in my Bidong room. The early evening light had turned the sea deep gold. Below us, new arrivals hurried down the jetty from a small fishing boat which rode so low beside the mooring barge that it looked ready to sink.

"Such a small boat," Cung said. "My boat I piloted from Vietnam to Malaysia was seventy-one feet. I brought on this small boat 687 people."

Seventy-one feet. Twice *Erma*'s length. For nearly seven hundred passengers. I looked with renewed respect at this slender man, who looked younger than his forty-five years. Although his hair was streaked with gray, his cheeks were smooth, his deep brown eyes almost naïvely trusting.

As Bidong's mayor, Cung worked tirelessly from dawn until midnight, handling both major concerns and petty details. Uncle often reminded me that when the toilets piled over during Tết and the sanitation workers refused to clean them because of the holiday, it was Cung who had rolled up his trousers and swabbed out the filth.

"How will we make it after Cung leaves?" Uncle said every day or so, looking more morose with each repetition. We both knew that any day Cung's name could be on a departure list.

Before he came to Bidong, Cung had been a heart surgeon and the head of Nguyễn Van Hoc Hospital in Saigon. On April 29, 1975, the day before the city fell, a group of doctors asked him for permission to escape and suggested he join them. The hospital, a Saigon government stronghold treating six hundred patients, was sustaining heavy mortar fire. Since Cung knew his entire medical staff would abandon the hospital if he did, he decided to remain. He was finishing heart surgery when the Communists arrived. They arrested him before he could accompany his patient to the recovery room.

These memories etched lines of weariness around Cung's eyes as he told me about the reeducation camp the Communists had put him in. His right leg became paralyzed while he was in the camp. Still, he worked on a construction team. From six in the morning until four or five in the afternoon he stood on one foot and sawed.

At one point, according to Cung, two men attempting escape had scrambled through the barbed wire. One was shot and severely wounded; guards left him in the sun and arrested the other man. Another time they locked two men in a metal supply container left by the Americans. During the day the container grew fiercely hot, at night bitterly cold. In Quảng Ngãi during the war, I'd observed Saigon and American soldiers also using those containers as prisons, sometimes locking up twenty to thirty people in one of them, and I often saw the bodies of Vietcong they'd left on the streets to rot.

Although Communist guards in Cung's camp said the two men would be released after a week, they forced the prisoners' friends to dig two long, deep holes. After one week, the guards led the men out of the supply container, escorted them to the ditches, and shot them in the presence of their friends. During six months on Bidong, I heard many reeducation camp stories of hard work for men who previously had not done manual labor. Only Cung's account mentioned violence.

Cung lived in the reeducation center for a year until the new government needed a heart specialist for Nguyen Van Hoc Hospital. After his release, he worked a year without salary and lived on sweet potatoes and water. During that time he performed operations while standing on his left leg, his right propped on a chair.

"I was a flamingo," he said.

During this period, some of Cung's friends who'd bought a boat asked him to lead them, and he agreed to do so. He located an old compass and a three-foot-square map of Southeast Asia. He cut the map into sections, which he hid inside the cover of the heart surgery textbook he had been writing for ten years.

"Everyone I knew was leaving," Cung said. "I didn't want to abandon my motherland, but my children—I didn't want my children to be watched."

"At night," he continued, "I took the compass and map, climbed onto the house roof. I study the stars until I know them as well as I know the heart. Then one night I dressed like a mechanic and escaped under the name of a Chinese."

I remembered hearing that Cung's boat had been one of the few to fight off pirates. "And pirates?" I asked.

He smiled with an impish grin. "I study about pirates." He drew a circle. "This is their strategy. The pirates make a ring, with seven or eight boats, five to ten miles in diameter. As soon as Vietnamese boat passes between pirate boats, the pirates close in."

Unknowingly, however, Cung piloted his boat into a pirate ring around noon on April 14. Another smaller refugee boat followed. Soon, an unfamiliar vessel, its sailors calling in friendly voices, approached Cung's boat. The thirsty, sweaty refugees scrambled for cakes of ice the strangers tossed to them. The boat people grabbed anchors the sailors threw onto their deck.

"Don't!" Cung shouted from the bridge. He ordered the anchor ropes cut. He spun the helm.

As Cung told this, his hand darted like a water snake. "How do you call it in English when a boat goes like this?" he asked.

"Tack," I said.

A second ship closed in from the other side. Cung took a new tack, then another until his boat slipped past the pirates. "But then," he said, and his face darkened, "they pursued the other refugee boat. I could not rescue."

Just before 10 P.M. that evening Cung noticed black shapes looming over a fluorescent sea. He pushed his boat to full throttle. He could smell her heavy exhaust and sense the fear spreading across her deck. The passengers wanted to surrender, but Cung refused, yelling that the pirates were angry from the earlier escape and would smash their boat and maim and kill.

"Besides," he shouted from the bridge, "the pirates are no more than fifty. We have seven hundred!" He sent the women and children into the center of the boat. He instructed the men to grab sticks and line the gunwales.

When the pirates tried to board, Cung signaled from the bridge. Yelling, the refugees beat off the intruders. Their wooden sticks clattered against the metal blades of fishing knives.

With Cung directing from the bridge, the Vietnamese fought on, slashing and shouting and striking as the pirates' boats bobbed next to theirs. For more than an hour they defended their boat until the pirates abandoned the attack. Then the Vietnamese put aside their sticks and bandaged their knife wounds. One respected elder in his seventies had fallen overboard; a five-year-old girl lay dead upon the deck.

The next morning Cung sighted Bidong, but motored past because the island's seaward side was wild. On April 15, 1979, at the end of the spring monsoon, he landed his people on mainland Malaysia.

"My wife wept when we stepped ashore and inside I wept, too. We hadn't wanted to leave our homeland. I didn't mind the hard life, but what future was there for my skills? We'd tried to stay.

"But we have children. They would always be suspect, never allowed university, never allowed a profession. So my wife and I, we left our home in Saigon for Bidong. From here we go to America. To Van Buren, Arkansas. There my sister lives. There I'll make every effort to study so that one beautiful day I can return home to serve my *quê hương*."

At the time of this conversation with Cung, while the darkening evening light filtered through my window, he and his family had been waiting on Bidong for nine months, listening with each movement list for their names to be called.

"Many tears at the jetty," Monika said one morning about three weeks later. Cung and his family were finally leaving for the States. On the mooring barge, he moved through the crowd, clasping the hands of friends while the new camp leader stood proudly by.

I was taking photographs. No matter how I changed my angle or distance, Uncle sidled into the center of every one of the many farewell shots of Cung. In each one Uncle grinned broadly.

After *Black Gold* had pulled away and those of us left behind on the mooring barge had finally stopped waving to Cung, I looked around. Uncle stood alone on the corner of the barge, sobbing and staring out to sea.

Bidong's jetty beach, spring 1980.

Islanders' houses framed out of bamboo cut from the mountainside.

A father sits with his children at the entrance to their house.
Hammocks woven from MRCS-issued twine held sleeping islanders
secure above the reach of the rats.

A vendor sells squid on a square of blue plastic.

Two vendors sell Western drugs and Chinese medicine.

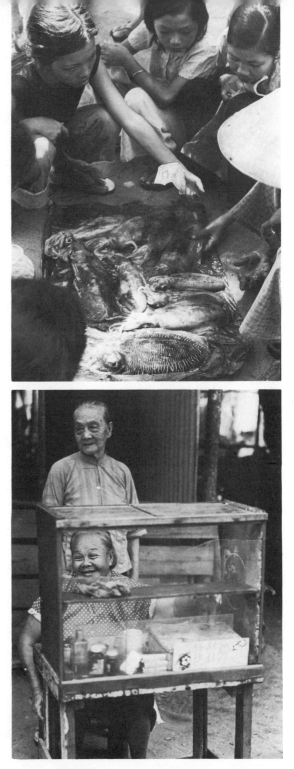

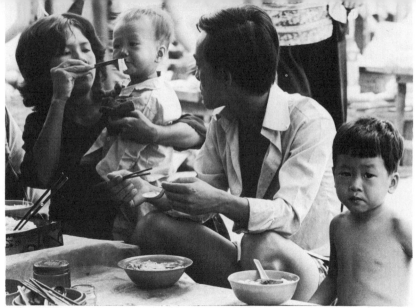

A family shares *pho*—a soup made of rice noodles—at a stall in the black market.

Two children sit on the steps of their house built on stilts over the main sewer.

Kim, age twelve, the island's only Amerasian child.

Children play with toy boats fashioned from ration tins.

A refugee boat approaches Bidong

New arrivals squat on the jetty to be counted. The curly-haired girl in the foreground was among a half dozen who collapsed as they walked down the pier.

Refugees carrving their life's possessions.

Expectant new arrivals at the end of their journey.

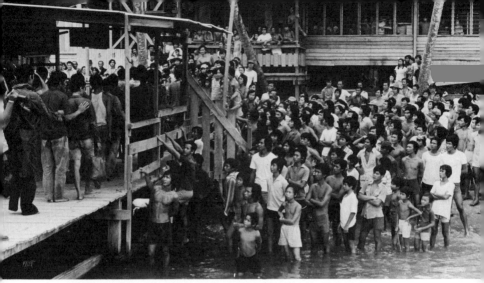

Islanders crowd the beach and hospital ward windows as they search for loved ones.

Children swim near the jetty. The beached metal boat, which brought over seven hundred people, was home for several families.

Craftsmen build fishing dinghies from plywood pilfered from MRCS supplies. They sold their catch in the morning black market.

A Buddhist nun makes "pigs' ears," a crisp coconut cookie, in the hut she shares with orphan children.

A dragon made from cardboard ration cartons and strings of pink hammock twine dances on a camp path during Tet.

Two "unaccompanied minors"—children whose parents remained in Vietnam—walk with me on the camp's main path. The path is almost empty because at midday the temperature approached 100 degrees. Photo by Peter Fleischl.

A girl hangs up laundry in her hut's backyard, which faces the main sewer. During the monsoon rains the sewer flooded the houses.

r. Tho (left) the day he
placed Dr. Thuan (right)
Head of the Health
ivision.

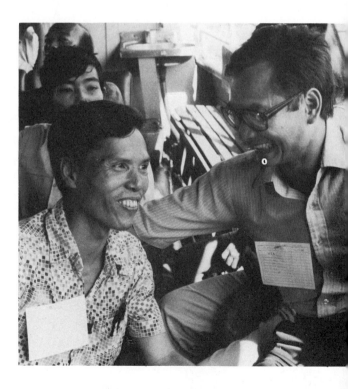

Dr. Cung, a lung specialist, stands with Duc, his replacement as camp leader, on the day of Cung's departure for the United States.

Thanh, age twelve, the girl who fell down an abandoned well in which neighbors had burned trash.

The prospect of starting a new life in Australia was frightening for this elderly couple.

"Mrs. Foot" (right) departs for Australia with her family.

Bidong at dusk.

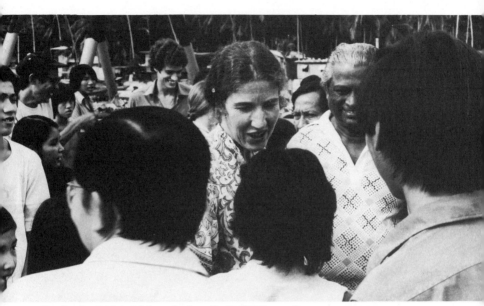

Uncle, the Indian Malay who handled MRCS supplies, accompanies me
as I say good-bye to friends on the day of my departure from the island.
Photo by Joe Stimpfl.

I was deeply touched by all those who saw me off, yet saddened that I would never see most of them again.

9
Fish Fight

On Bidong, fresh food was treasure. A year before I lived on the island, MRCS had tried sending fish. It warmed on the Trengganu pier during loading, stagnated in a hold during transit, and rotted on the Bidong jetty during unloading. A year later, people were still talking about the stench.

Late one night a week after Cung's departure, two young fishermen who'd harvested their nets in Vietnamese waters, then taken off for Malaysia, landed on Bidong with an estimated three tons of fish, on ice.

The word "Fish!" spread through the sleeping camp like wind before a storm. People surged down the dark, twisting paths to the beach. They ran through the jetty gate, their feet pounding the planks as they dashed toward the newly arrived boat. Uncle slammed the gate and called back those who'd already pushed through, but they only ran faster. Snapping whips, the Malaysian guards shoved Vietnamese off the jetty, but the word "Fish!" spread; more people jostled against the gate. The guards pointed their guns at the pressing Vietnamese and cocked the triggers. Uncle bellowed in a voice that carried over the noisy crowd. He bellowed again and again until the crowd dispersed.

Then Uncle gathered up as many fish as he could hold in his arms. "For my friends," he said.

"No, Uncle," I said.

"For my friends!" He stomped off, fish tails waggling against his abdomen.

I was furious with Uncle for this pilfering. We didn't speak for days, and the next morning he was conspicuously absent from the wharf.

Early in the morning, longshoremen started loading the catch into large wicker baskets, which they winched up out of the hold and dumped onto the mooring barge. Dục, the new camp leader, stood in the middle of the huge pile, dividing it into seven smaller ones for the seven camp zones. While Dục sorted, looters grabbed fish and scurried across the barge toward the jetty gangplank, where I was waiting for them. Each looter I apprehended protested that Dục or Selva, the MRCS staffperson who handled supply orders, had granted him a special favor.

Division heads rushed onto the jetty. They all argued with Dục while the zone leaders continued to haggle with each other. When the division heads asked Dục to provide special rations for their staffs, the zone chiefs pushed them aside and started to divide the pile themselves.

Selva shooed more looters toward the gangplank, but they slipped back into the press of arms and hands reaching into piles of fish. A man clutched two tunas to his chest and ran. Bumping into me, he smashed the fish between us, nearly dropping them. The MRCS social workers protested when Selva took fish they'd grabbed. He tossed the fish back into the pile and sent the social workers off the jetty, but the moment Selva turned away, they circled back into the crowd. Angry, I ushered them off the wharf.

Duc, his new camp leader badge bright in the sun, argued with zone chiefs and division heads, whose hands were slick with scales and guts. Duc's voice rose in pitch. The sun glared down, melting the ice and warming the fish. It was hot, greasy hot. The baskets crossing the gangplank on their way to the zones smelled of fish. The men carrying them stank of fish. I stank. Everything began to reek of rotting fish.

Selva stepped onto the deck and peered into the hold. Immediately he clamped his nose, then clasped his stomach and jumped off the boat. He ran down the mooring barge until he stopped, leaning over the water, hands on his quivering abdomen. When he straightened, his dark Indian face was greenish.

We agreed to dump the rest of the cargo at sea. Duc threw rotting fish back onto the deck of the boat while Selva cleared everyone from the barge. However, none of us could catch the swimmers. Their hands darted up onto the barge as they pulled fish back into the sea. They clasped the fish to their chests and, kicking, swam with them under the deep green water. Duc shouted, I shouted, even gentle Selva shouted.

Once the last fish had been dumped back onto the vessel, Selva fetched a Malay captain to drive the boat with him and the fish out to sea. As the boat pulled away and the sound of her engine faded, I could see Selva moving aft away from the cargo. He leaned over the deck railing, limp and pale, staring glumly down into the passing waves.

The mooring barge was quiet. Fish guts coated the rusted metal, which glittered in the sun. Waves with a surface film of scales flicked against its iron sides. Two dead tunas lay on the rocky bottom far below.

I started to walk down the jetty, but then turned around for a moment to look back. Dục, the new camp leader, stood alone on the barge amid the scales and guts. His shoulders slumped. His white shirt was spotted, and his new red badge was smudged. He held his wet, slimy hands away from his sides.

⟐ 10

In Transit

A piercing scream awoke me. I sat up in an unfamiliar bed and swung my legs out into empty space. For a moment, I didn't know where I was. Then I remembered. I was accompanying a transfer of the island's retarded, disabled, and mentally ill to Kuala Lumpur. The UN staff thought they could resettle the handicapped more easily if they could visit them regularly in the capitol. It was our first night en route, and we were bedded down in Marang Transit Camp, which had once been a seaside hotel operated by the sultan of Trengganu State. Our dormitory had been the grand reception hall.

In a huge, shadowy room filled with huddled sleeping figures, I was sitting on the upper deck of a bunk missing half its slats. I reached out and touched the wall. Paint peeled off in huge flakes. Climbing down, I slipped into my rubber sandals and went to investigate the screaming. I crossed between rows of bunks to the other side of the room, where I found a teenage boy slamming his fist into his jaw. The boy's face was puffy. An enlarged tongue filled his mouth. Drool slid down his chin. His mother held onto his wrists, restraining him, but still he beat at his jaw.

"A toothache," she said.

Thinking codeine might make him sleep, I fetched cough syrup from the first-aid kit. As the mother held her son's head in her lap, I spooned the medicine into his mouth. She clamped his nose and raised his chin while I stroked his throat until he swallowed. She rubbed the thick, red syrup into his gums. Soon he settled.

After three months on Bidong, I'd come to feel as if I belonged there. Now, as I returned to bed, I felt uprooted and lonely. In the bunk below me, three sisters nestled around each other. The lips of the oldest sister moved in her sleep, making a purple growth on her cheek quiver. Her baby slept in a hammock hanging from my bunk.

I stretched out on the boards, which felt smooth and cool against my sunburn. Mosquitoes droned, nipping my ears before they flew off. On the ceiling, a four-inch gecko jerked its head as it snatched a mosquito. The tiny lizard strutted along graffiti—names and boat numbers scrawled over names and boat numbers—that previous tenants had inked onto the green paint. Pausing on "Nguyen thi Thuyet DN 6082," it made a guttural crow that pervaded the murmuring sounds of slumber.

A sudden puff of wind filled the room with the scent of the sea. The tiny pink hammock below me swayed. In the darkness grazed by frail moonlight, our bunk and all those bunks around it seemed to sway like a fleet of boats at anchor.

The morning sun lifted from the horizon, spreading waves of rose light over the sea. Its rays caught in the spirals of wire encircling Marang camp and ignited the barbs into red sparks. It warmed the clusters of people who sat on their bulging gunnysacks under the palm trees. Even though departure was scheduled for midmorning, they'd risen at 4 A.M., their excited whispers animating the bunkroom.

We loaded. Kuan Ying, a MRCS social worker, handed out to each person a carton of tea, a slab of bread, and two eggs. Trained in England as a midwife, Kuan Ying was a Malaysian of Chinese ancestry. She was a pretty woman with delicate features and a complexion that was almond gold except for splotches on her neck. These, the result of a pigment deficiency, were as white as the inside of an almond. Her hands, which had been affected by the same pigment loss, looked as if she wore white gloves.

While Kuan Ying handed out the food, I checked the group's identification papers against the yellow card pinned to the shirt of each Head of Family. HANDICAPPED was stamped over the names. The passengers boarded the buses, wedging sacks under the seats. Kuan Ying rode on one bus, I another. As we drove away, the children leaned out the windows and waved to the lone Malay guard lounging in the doorway to an empty bunkroom.

The road ran south along the sea. Stilt houses with goats dozing underneath bordered the beach. The night before, offshore lights had dipped in the darkness as fishermen harvested their nets. Now they spread their catch into a rose carpet in the sun. The rich aroma of roasting prawns surrounded their houses.

I daydreamed as the miles sped past. I dozed. Shifting, I dozed again. For three hours we drove past the sea and the gray clapboard houses until we reached Kuantan, a sleepy seaside town. Then we turned west toward the mountains.

As we drove, my mind wandered. These were the first hours in weeks that I'd had simply to sit. Suddenly I felt homesick. I realized that since coming to Bidong I'd missed

the quickening pulse of a life on the road, the smoothness of a
steering wheel in my palms, the race of a motor at the touch
of my foot. I missed the smell of gasoline and the slipperiness
of motor oil, but most of all I missed the kids on my bus.

In Quảng Ngãi ten years before, I had driven toddlers to
and from the Quaker Day Care Center. One day I had
counted six hundred army trucks and forty tanks roaring past
me on the dusty one-mile stretch of Phan Bội Châu Street.
With a shudder I saw that as a taxpayer, I had paid for those
armaments. I decided that when I returned to the United
States, I would try to earn so little that I wouldn't have to pay
taxes for war.

After I came back from Vietnam in 1971, I moved to the
hills of Appalachian Ohio and found a job driving a school bus
there. For ten years I rode along the dirt lanes that twisted
through the Ohio hills, stopping at small family farms on the
ridgetops and at coal company settlements in the hollows.
Each morning, in two hours, I picked up ten riders for a
special district-wide school. All tested below 50 IQ; most had
physical handicaps and some were disruptive.

Wayne was one of my passengers. He was in his mid-twenties. Winter or summer he wore bright red suspenders and an
aviator's cap with its fur ear flaps down. Although he was
almost blind, he liked nothing better than to watch Westerns
on television. I was a disappointment to Wayne because I
didn't have a TV, but one day I found I had something to talk
about that was of great interest to him.

I'd brought some heifers back from a stock sale. The heifers
stampeded off the truck, charged through the barnyard
fence, and bolted straight down the hollow, knocking out the
line fence before they disappeared over the countryside.

Every afternoon for six weeks, my neighbors and I chased one or another of those cows.

Every morning as soon as he boarded, Wayne would say, "Rounded up them heifers yet? You know what you oughta do, Wady? You know what you oughta do?" He'd repeat the question until I responded No.

"Saddle up that old gray mare and lassoo 'em." At that point he'd strap down his aviator's cap, snap his suspenders, and for the rest of the route bounce in his seat as if it were a saddle.

"You know what you oughta do, Wady?" Wayne said when, after six weeks, I finally announced a completed roundup. "You know what you oughta do to keep 'em from running away again?"

I shook my head.

"Put glue on their heels!"

I counted on Wayne to remind me about all sorts of details and to take care of George, his seatmate. The two of them sat directly behind me. George was twelve and he wore diapers that made him waddle. He couldn't talk, but his shriek was as piercing as a hawk's. Usually George carried a ball, which he held on to fiercely, picking holes in its red rubber.

Once when we were driving at 50 mph, the ball bounced across the aisle and into the stairwell. George screeched. His wailing cut into my ears. He snatched my hair in his talon grip and yanked, whipping my neck against the seat back. My hands jerked at the wheel; my feet groped for pedals. Pinned, I could see only the ceiling. I felt the bus swerve out of control before I could stop it.

The pressure on my neck suddenly released. When I sat up and looked around, George was laughing. He picked bits of white foam off the Styrofoam cup that Wayne had given him as a substitute for the ball. The bus, idling on the wrong shoulder on the wrong side of an empty highway, pointed down an embankment toward the Hocking River.

"You know what you oughta do, Wady?" Wayne popped his suspenders.

I pulled the emergency brake. My knees were quivering and my armpits burned with sudden sweat.

"You know what you oughta do?"

"No."

"You could tie up that hair."

Every morning thereafter, when George's mother led him onto the bus, Wayne would pluck his red suspenders and say, "You know what you oughta do, Wady?"

"Yes, Wayne," I'd answer. I'd wind my hair around my fingers and tuck it into a knot at the nape of my neck the way a Vietnamese friend had taught me years before in Quảng Ngãi.

The community on our school bus was a fragile one easily cracked by a new rider. The first afternoon seven-year-old Jon joined us, he removed all his clothes. Jon was a powerfully built child who communicated in grunts. I was watching the road when he threw his jeans, shirt, one shoe and his undershorts out the window. They landed on the bus roof.

"He's naked, he's naked," Janine chanted, pointing to Jon. Janine had both her adult and her baby teeth and she said everything twice.

Jon spat on the floor when I pulled off the road, and he spat at me when I rose to retrieve his clothes.

"Bull's-eye!" Wayne cheered.

Indeed, Jon was a good shot. Spittle hit me between the eyes and slid off the bridge of my nose. It ran down my cheeks like tears.

Jon beat the side of the bus. He grabbed George's ball and threw it at the windshield. It ricocheted and hit Ivy on the shoulder. Ivy cried. George screeched with his mouth open so far that I could see his tonsils.

It was a sunny day in the early fall and the leaves were just turning. Immediately I started up the bus and, without saying anything, drove until we passed under a low-hanging branch that swept the garments off the roof. I retrieved the clothes and held them in my lap until Jon's house. Perhaps I was cruel to make Jonathan Burke Whittson ride the rest of that route bare-bottomed and clad in one shoe but then, although he sprang other tricks, he never repeated that one.

If one person could crack our fragile community, one word could shatter it. Maureen knew best how to utter that word. Her victim was usually Ivy, a bearlike sixteen-year-old. When happy, Ivy hugged with rib-cracking gusto; when distressed, she swatted. Maureen, who was six years younger, was a Downs-syndrome child. One day, when I was watching the road, she slipped between seats until she sat directly behind Ivy.

"Baby," Maureen hissed.

"I ain't no baby!" Ivy cried.

"In your seat, Maureen!" I directed. I was on the main street of town and the traffic in front of me was as demanding as the fracas behind.

"Baby. Baby." Maureen's voice was barely audible.

"Ao-ooh!" Ivy howled. She swatted George, who let loose a shriek, which he held at a piercing decibel.

"He's too noisy!" Ivy complained.

"Quiet, all of you!" I yelled. A car was tailgating me. I couldn't stop.

"Baby, baby. Said it, said it," Janine chanted.

"Shut up," said Rose, an adult who worked as custodian in a local laundromat.

Jonathan Burke Whittson beat the side of the bus, which

resounded like a snare drum. Then he farted, releasing the scent of warm feces.

"Ah-ooooh!" Ivy grabbed the tails of her jacket and pulled it up her back and over her head like a tent.

By then Maureen had slipped back to her own seat. She sat up straight, her tongue filling her satisfied grin. Next to Maureen, four-year-old Chelsea stared from her baby basket. Ronny Leen smiled through his drool. Danny, who had cerebral palsy, looked calmly out a window, his size-nine left foot propped on his size-six right.

I often leaned on Danny's calm. He was my first pickup and we had a half-hour ride alone together before the second person boarded. On clear mornings Danny, who was fourteen, would sing to the sun at the first sight of gold behind the hills:

Good morning, sun, good morning, sky.
Good morning, little birds that fly.
How did you know that it was day
And that the night had gone away?
Now I'm awake, I'm up now, too
I'll be right out to play with you.

And in the afternoons we'd sing about the milk goat who drank from a frozen stream and afterward only gave ice cream.

Often Danny would show me his notebook where he practiced writing his name. He knew that I wrote between bus routes, and we sometimes spoke about this. In fact, it was Danny with whom I talked most often that winter before I left for Bidong. At the end of my worst week Danny gave me a piece of bubble gum.

"Open it," he said.

I read the comic aloud to him.

"Now the fortune," he said.

"You will grow up to write fortunes for bubble gum."

"See!" Laughing, Danny flicked the tassle on my wool cap. He climbed off the bus, limped through the snow to his house, where he turned and waved.

During the weeks of transition before I left for Malaysia, I stayed close to my kids on the bus and to the other drivers, all women. For years we drivers had gathered every morning for breakfast when half our day's wage-earning work was done. I'll be okay, I often thought as Jonathan tested me, if I can just make it to breakfast.

We called each other by our CB handles. There was Bouncer, formerly the warden at the county jail; spicy Honeybear and tangy Sugarbee; quiet, plucky Banjo; Masher, who'd penetrate to any discussion's crucial point; and myself, nicknamed Mittens, because I was always wrapped in scarves. When the others said "book," they meant a magazine, and when they said "story," they meant a bawdy joke; yet the tales they recounted from their lives displayed more insight delivered with sharper twists of language than any classic I'd read. Day after day, year after year, as our personal lives cracked and broke apart and mended, we pulled into Ryan's Restaurant on Union Street, circled it with our yellow school buses and gathered around our usual table in the corner.

"Going to Malaria, are ya?" Sugarbee said when I told the drivers about leaving for Malaysia.

"Bring us back real coffee and bus stories," Masher said.

Now, heading into the Genting Highlands of Malaysia, the driver of our bus whipped over hills and around curves, speeding on the fringe of recklessness, bending forward over the wheel and continuously pressing the horn as if it were the accelerator. The wheels of the bus barely grazed the pavement as it careened from one side of the highway to the other, passing lumber trucks.

I gripped the edge of the seat in front of me. The black hair of a child with cerebral palsy brushed my wrist. The teenager with the toothache banged his head against the window. Each knock made a sharp cracking sound that reverberated through my bones. His mother wedged cardboard against the glass, muffling the crack into a thud.

It was a diaperless ride for the incontinent. At crucial moments their parents held them over the aisle. Even with the windows open, the humid air hung over us, drawing sweat like a sauna and uniting us in intimacy.

In the Quảng Ngãi van, only the driver's window opens. Forty day-care children press forward toward that one source of ventilation. They hang about my neck like warm, moist slugs. Their damp hair touches my cheeks. They pluck my curls, pulling the coils to full extension, giggling when they spring back.

It's my last evening bus run for the Day Care Center before I return to the United States. In front with me sits Xuân Lan, who's the Center director. She holds a paraplegic toddler injured by a mine; next to her sits the toddler's younger brother, whose legs are peppery with embedded shrapnel. Two more teachers and forty-one kids are crammed into the back: the van's stern sinks and its bow rises. Like a blunt-nosed launch, it plows through traffic.

The kids sing a lilting melody about the sugar cane bird, a tiny creature smaller than a chicadee. It's a culinary delicacy particular to Quảng Ngãi province. Once Xuân Lan served me whole fried sugar cane bird—a single clogging mouthful

*of head and beak, feathers and feet. I prefer singing about
sugar cane birds to eating them, and I prefer that song to the
kids' favorite, which bothers me. Once more as they start to
sing it, I express my discontent to Xuân Lan.*

*"Vietnam's had a thousand years under the Chinese," she
yells over the children's singing.*

*"But do we have to teach violence to three-year-olds?" I
ask.*

"Exterminate the Chinese!" the children sing.

*"Một tay!—One fist!" they shout. Hands shoot upward and
the bus sways to the right.*

"Hai tay!—Two fists!" We veer to the left.

*"Một chân! Hai chân!—One foot! Two!" The bus lurches
with the stomping.*

*We plow into a mud wallow. The sow lolling in it refuses to
move, but when I lean on the horn, which bleats like a nanny
goat, she lumbers out. Bicycles and motorcycles swirl around
us while the pony carts proceed at their own leisurely pace.
Tanks and trucks rumble past.*

*That day, as usual, we stop along Phan Bội Châu Street.
The kids tumble from the bus and run around to the one
open window. Child by child they come forward and bow
with arms folded across their chests.*

*"Chào Cô Lý đi về. Chào Cô Lý đi về.—Good-bye, Miss Lý,
you're leaving," each child murmurs before scampering
away.*

They're gone from my life, I thought, as I stared out the
window at Malaysian rain forests speeding past. They'd be
teenagers now, draft age. Who knows if they're even alive.

We were climbing a hill. Along the road, giant trees
loomed over a dense undergrowth of ferns and bamboo. We
swerved to the right around a truck carrying a single huge

tree trunk. Together, our bus and that truck broke over the crest.

"*Trời ơi!*—Oh, heavens!" An old woman gasped the loudest. Another bus was speeding directly toward us.

We swerved off the road, dodging, horn screeching. The other bus roared by.

"*Chết rồi!*—Dead already!" the old woman said.

Our bus wobbled along a ravine filled with feathery bamboo. When it lurched back onto the road, a boy without arms rolled off his seat. Before his mother could help him back up, he floundered in the spilled tea, eggshells, and urine.

"Too crowded," the man next to me said. His left eye wandered.

I edged farther toward the aisle.

"Too crowded," he said again. He'd muttered those words all during the trip. People said he'd repeated them endlessly on Bidong.

It wasn't until we reached the far side of the mountains that we stopped at a restaurant. The proprietor was ready. His tables were laden with fried bananas, sticky rice wrapped in leaves, star fruits, and slivers of melon. He was a swarthy Chinese man who held his hands together as he bowed to the new arrivals. Outside his restaurant stood a pile of durians, large prickly fruit the size and color of small watermelons. Malaysians consider them a delicacy, yet find their smell offensive.

The bus drivers, four of them for the two buses, winked at the proprietor. They greeted him warmly in Malay and sat at an outside table upwind of the durians. The proprietor presented them with dinners of rice and stewed goat.

Kuan Ying and I sat with people from her bus at a long table inside the restaurant. With her red fingernails Kuan Ying plucked apart a durian.

"Here," she said, handing me a piece of pulpy fruit as pale as her albino hands, "but hold your nose." The fruit was deeply succulent, sweet, and soft.

All around us, the passengers' voices grew animated as they savored fresh fruit and sticky rice. Soon the tables—which a few minutes earlier had looked so tidy—filled with thorny durian rinds, discarded banana leaves, empty soda bottles, and cigarette butts. A hunchback, who was bent over himself like a question mark, rose to pay his bill.

"Three dollars five," the proprietor said in English, signaling with his fingers. He stood behind a counter, his change box open before him.

With two hands the hunchback presented four bills. On Bidong, there was no change; everything there sold for multiples of one ringgit. The hunchback held out his right hand and rested his left on his youngest son's head, waiting for change.

"No change," the owner said. He pointed to the empty compartments as he deposited all four bills in his cash box. "So sorry." The change box clanked shut.

"How come you have no change," the hunchback answered in Vietnamese. He rose in height, his frame straightening toward an exclamation point.

"Very sorry," the proprietor said. "So very sorry."

Outside the door, the drivers eating near the pile of durians snickered. With the fingertips of their right hands they swept grains of rice together and popped the food into their mouths.

"Whenever you have refugees, you have vultures who feed off them," Kuan Ying muttered, dropping a durian skin on the floor. She rose and stepped on the rind, mashing its thorns into pulpy flesh. The offensive odor of durian rose with her.

"What do you mean, 'no change'!" she said in English. She switched to a tumble of Malay followed by Cantonese as rapid as buckshot. She glared. The heat of the trip had smudged her makeup so that her eyes glowered from ghostly white sockets in her golden face. She took paper and pencil from her bag. "Now we'll just set this straight. Give me those four ringgit."

The owner opened his cashbox and returned the money. He stood pressing his palms together and shuffling as Kuan Ying started a list on her piece of paper.

She wrote, "$3.05." Then she returned one ringgit to the hunchback and with a flick of her red-tipped fingers, motioned him and his family toward the buses.

The proprietor's frown darkened as Kuan Ying's list grew with each family's departure from the litter-strewn tables. He pushed his fists deep into his pockets. There was the sound of jingling change. Quickly he withdrew his hands.

I paid our bill, $1.05, with change I'd brought. My five-cent piece clattered when the proprietor dropped it into his empty box. The drivers rose and slipped away, but on the far side of the durians they stopped to whisper among themselves. Without glancing at the proprietor, they returned to their table, where each left a crumpled ringgit by his place.

Kuan Ying added the passengers' ringgit to her pile and recorded each charge in her column of figures. She tallied the bill and counted the money.

"Two ringgit short," she announced, bringing out her envelope of discretionary funds. "We'll have a petty snack on MRCS."

The drivers were gunning their engines. They stared grimly through their windshields as we counted noses. Then they slammed the doors and, locking their horns into a monotonic blare, stomped on the accelerators. As the buses lurched back onto the highway, the passengers stared through the windows at the proprietor standing alone behind his counter. Only one hand among the passengers waved. It was from the bus in the lead, and it was ghostly white with nails of sharp red.

As we drove on, the mountains and their forests of dense undergrowth disappeared behind us. We passed through villages with small shops displaying large overhead signs in Malay and Chinese. Women sauntered along the road. Men in sarongs squatted in the dust, tinkering with motorcycle engines. Goats with swaying udders snuffled through piles of rubbish.

The towns became city. As dusk settled, we entered Kuala Lumpur. Stocky cement structures gave way to steel and plate glass buildings that disappeared above our heads; our horn's scream joined the alarum of Asian commuters. Traffic spun around us and we spun around it until the first red light. There, everything stopped. Perpendicular lanes wedged together, jamming the intersection. The drivers seethed and their passengers steamed in heat heavy with fumes.

"Too crowded," my seatmate muttered.

"How abundant," said a woman with a shriveled arm.

Darkness settled as we drove out of the city and toward Sungei Besi Camp, where the handicapped and their families would be interned until Western countries accepted them.

The buses unloaded outside a chain-link fence. Although all the Malaysian camps were prisons, Bidong—like Alcatraz —was so isolated by the sea that the Malaysian guards had encased only their own compound in barbed wire. In contrast, this camp in Kuala Lumpur had five strands of wire on top of the chain link. A spotlight beam glanced through the fence, projecting a closely laced shadow fringed with barbs. Inside the camp, treeless red dust surrounded a tight grid of trailers. Designed for Scandinavia, the trailers had black roofs, tiny windows, and no air-conditioning. People sitting in the dust outside these houses wiped their foreheads on their sleeves. They fanned each other with pack ration cardboard.

I stood opposite a Malay policeman at the gate, watching the passengers from Bidong drag their gunnysacks toward the fenced compound. They stood in line before the policeman, who scrutinized their papers before he let them in.

"Good-bye," I said to my seatmate. "May you find strength and joy in your new life."

"Too crowded," he muttered.

The hunchback leaned over his children, and the old woman with the shriveled arm pushed to be next. The young woman with the purple growth on her cheek shifted her son to her other hip as the guard checked her papers. Once through the gate, she turned and waved. She took the baby's hand in hers and waved it at me. The mother whose teenager had a toothache was the last in line. She stopped in front of me. In her left hand she clutched a cooking pot full of clothes, rice, tea, and two sticks of incense. With the other she supported her son.

"*Chào Cô Lý đi về*—Good-bye, Miss Lý, you're leaving," the mother said, bowing. "May you and your family always enjoy good health, prosperity, and happiness." She passed through the gate and crossed the chain-link shadow. The policeman closed the gate behind her and flipped the latch, which fell with a definitive clink. He inserted a padlock and snapped it shut.

11
An Island on the Mainland

RADIO NEWS FROM TRENGGANU. 2:30 P.M. Prepare for new arrivals: sixteen survivors of a pirated boat that left Vietnam with seventy-six on board.

RADIO NEWS FROM TRENGGANU. 4 P.M. Washed ashore on the mainland: three bodies and one head.

The sixteen survivors came on *Black Gold* just at sunset. They stood along the deck railing, staring at us as the World War II landing craft inched alongside the mooring barge. Their faces were drawn, exhausted, their hair stiff with salt. One man had blood seeping through a bandage that was wrapped around his brow. He touched his wife's shoulder. A teenage boy stood alone, his eyes glazed as he stared over the rail.

The entire camp turned out to meet the survivors. Hands reached out to help them cross the gangplank from the mooring barge to the jetty. Empty-handed, the new arrivals stayed close to each other during the long walk down the jetty to the beach.

A few nights later I went to wake a patient who was to make the journey to the mainland hospital for observation. Hai was a woman in her fifties who had a cardiac condition as well as a goiter that rose like a hill from her neck. She lay asleep on a cot at the far end of the Bidong general ward. Her gray hair was thin at the temples. When she inhaled, I could just see in the dim light the tip of her gold tooth. Her toothless seven-year-old granddaughter slept curled inside Hai's arms. I touched Hai's shoulder gently, trying not to wake the sleeping child.

Just as Hai and I reached the jetty, the generator hesitated, then quieted. All along the beach, fluorescent lights flickered as the camp settled into moon dappled darkness. At the end of the jetty, waves lapped against *Red Crescent 2* bobbing at her creaking lines. *RC 2* had to leave deep in the night in order to reach the treacherous Trengganu River channel by high tide at dawn.

Hai, who'd decided to travel without the usual family member as escort, peered into *RC 2*'s cabin. There, three Malay boatmen slept flopped over each other like fish in a hold, sarongs loose around their hips, their chests bare.

"Sợ quá.—Fearful," Hai said. She stepped backward and clutched her sack of possessions. Her fingers picked at the sack's woven pink twine.

"I'll go with you," I said. I awakened the captain, who cast off and cranked the engine.

Hai and I sat forward in the bow, our blouses billowing in the breeze. As *RC 2* eased into the darkness, the rubbish barge with its wafting odor of rotting garbage merged with the beach. The shore receded into darkness. Soon even Bidong's volcanic cone disappeared. The breeze stiffened. We shivered and turned up our collars.

"Would you rather ride in the cabin?" I asked.

Hai shook her head. The wind lifted a strand of gray hair escaping from the bun at the nape of her neck.

"Maybe they have a blanket." I grasped the winching boom and scrambled aft to the cabin.

The captain stood near his sleeping crew as he rolled the helm slowly to starboard and back to port. I gestured toward a blanket behind him. He stayed the helm with his toe and reached for it. Offering a life jacket, he made a pillow with his hands and mimicked a snore, then laughed, the stub of his cigarette wagging on his lip.

In the bow, Hai and I stuffed the life jacket behind our backs. We draped the blanket over us and leaned back against the bulwark.

"Perhaps you fear the sea after your trip from Vietnam," I said, pulling the blanket closer around my shoulders. I was grateful that it enclosed Hai's warmth too.

"No. We had water. And no pirates." Hai touched her goiter. "But—but the sea makes me long for Vietnam." She looked eastward toward the moon. As far as one could see, moonlight glittered in patterns like silver flying fish gliding over the waves.

Nestling like rice bowls, Hai and I curled around each other and slept. We awakened when the sky was gray-orange. Ahead lay the Trengganu River estuary with great swells thrusting between sand spits. A crew member scrambled forward and stood gazing intently on either side of the hull's stem. He signaled with his hands, and the captain maneuvered *RC 2* through the snaking channel. On one shoal listed the Singapore tanker that had run aground months before; on the other rested ribs from the wrecked Vietnamese boat.

Malaysian craft left the river as we slipped in. Nets piled their bows, while astern, bare-chested fishermen stood smoking in bright orange sarongs. Once through the estuary, *RC 2* eased into the Trengganu jetty. We climbed onto the pier as a Chinese cyclo driver pedaled up, ringing his bell. He raised the trishaw's accordion top when Hai and I climbed inside. The muscles of the driver's calves bulged taut as he pedaled uphill through the Chinese market. Merchants were sliding back their iron gates and arranging displays of chopsticks and woks, shrimp and garlic.

At the hospital, an orderly led us to the women's ward, a long stucco building under the flame trees. *"Đẹp quá!*—So beautiful!" Hai said as we entered the ward. Wildly patterned curtains fluttered in windows along the walls. The beds had mattresses and the sheets were stark white. The women who stared from row upon row of beds all wore stark white overshirts and green sarongs.

A Malay nurse brought Hai a set of hospital clothes. She showed her how to hold one end of the sarong against her abdomen, wrap the material around her hips, fold the other end and tuck it in at her waist. She pointed to the bathroom and then to Hai's *quần*.

In Quảng Ngãi we used to call *quần* "slimy slacks." These loosely fitting satin trousers, commonly worn by Vietnamese peasants, had a slippery texture. The satin felt cool, and the black color was practical. On Bidong I wore my old *quần* with barbed-wire nicks from daily use ten years before in Quảng Ngãi; sometimes in the States I had worn them when I needed to be dressy.

Hai glanced at her satin trousers and set the net bundle aside on her bed. With two hands she politely accepted the garments. She touched her goiter and looked around the ward at the women in green sarongs, who watched her as she walked down the long aisle between the rows of beds. When Hai returned, she held her *quần* in one hand and with the other anxiously clutched the bright green tuck at her waist. She looked back and forth at the rows of beds from which Malay, Indian and Chinese occupants watched her. She sat on her own cot and stared bleakly at the floor.

"Hai ơi! Hai ơi!" Bidong patients called out. They were peering between the flowered curtains in the windows.

Hai looked up and laughed, her gold tooth shining.

The Bidong patients invited Hai to the hospital canteen, where they bought her coffee and sweet rolls with ringgit given them by a Malaysian patient of Chinese ethnic origin. They asked her question after question about news of the island.

While on the mainland a week later, I stopped by the hospital to see Hai. It was evening. Children played tag in the hospital courtyard while women in green sarongs chatted nearby. Three goats walked past me, their hooves clattering on the concrete walkway. In the women's ward, Hai brimmed with news. The doctors had discharged her. Her gold tooth brightened her smile as she touched her goiter and asked for transport to Bidong.

On the next bed sat the seventeenth survivor of the pirated boat that had left Vietnam with seventy-six on board. Her name was Khen. Khen's face was black, the skin on her cheeks cracked like a shattered windshield. Her lips and tongue were so swollen that she winced as she spoke the pleasantries required by Hai's introduction.

By now I knew the terrible story of Khen's voyage. While her boat was at sea, a pirate vessel with eight men on board had approached. The pirates threw anchors, hooking the gunwales of the Vietnamese craft, but when they tried to board, the Vietnamese resisted. The Thais threw rags soaked in diesel fuel. They were preparing torches when the Vietnamese hurled gasoline back at them.

The pirates summoned another Thai vessel, which sped toward the Vietnamese boat. Engines roaring, it rammed the Vietnamese craft, splitting her hull into two. Passengers screamed as they fell into the sea. They floundered, grabbing shreds of planking and empty petrol cans. The waves became glassy with the purple tint of spreading diesel. The Thais fished Vietnamese from the water. Brandishing knives, they chopped off their heads and threw the heads back into the sea: the water turned blood red.

For three days, Khen had clung to a piece of planking. Finally, a Malaysian trawler had picked her up and brought her into Trengganu.

I didn't talk with Khen during that visit, since I knew she'd already been besieged by journalists and UN staff seeking her story. But I did offer to mail a letter for her, because Malaysian guards took three months to censor Vietnamese mail whereas letters I posted took one week. Hai clicked her tongue against her gold tooth at my suggestion. She knew the guards forbade MRCS staff to mail letters for islanders.

Khen shook her head No. She looked down at her hands, which were puffy with white cracks splitting the blackened skin.

"Too hard to write," she said.

"Maybe Hai could write for you," I said just before I left the ward.

Later, in the courtyard, I visited with other Bidong patients. They were excited to receive the letters I'd brought from their families on the island. As we chatted, Hai crossed the grill of shadows. After a week in Trengganu, she wore her green sarong with the ease of a Malay. In one hand she carried a letter, which was addressed from Khen to Toronto.

Cuong joined us. He was the young man tending the child who had fallen down the well. "So much has happened since I last saw you," he said. "We lost Quảng, and then his wife got sick. Now there is the survivor of the pirated boat."

Hai described how Cuổng had fed Khen when her tongue was so swollen she couldn't sip. He had sucked milk into a straw and plugged the end with his forefinger. Then leaning over Khen, who lay motionless on her bed, he'd carefully pried apart her cracked lips. Slipping the straw into her mouth, he released the milk a few drops at a time. Every two hours he returned to feed Khen in this manner until she could drink.

"And Thanh?" I asked, remembering how a month earlier Cuổng and I had peered between flowered curtains at the severely burned child.

"When they change her bandages," Cưổng said, glancing around the circle at Hai and the others, "our hearts turn upside down."

The next morning I bought pineapples in the Trengganu market for the hospital patients and a Malay phrase book for Cưổng. He was brushing back Thanh's hair when I entered her ward. She lay at the far end of a long row of beds filled with patients all wearing green sarongs and white overshirts.

Cưổng smiled and moved a chair near the injured child. That was the closest I'd been to Thanh since she lay shrieking, terribly burned, in the Bidong hospital. Her sarong concealed the dressings on her right thigh and leg; bandages covered her right arm and hand. The fingers of her right hand protruded at stark angles from the white gauze.

When I started to introduce myself, Thanh took my hand in her good one and stopped me, saying she remembered the day we'd met. Her face was fresh and her complexion was golden except for a yellow burn spot on one cheek. Her Vietnamese tones were clear and soothing, and her few English words were crisp.

Cuổng cut a pineapple into wedges so yellow that they looked artificially colored. Sweet juice dripped from our hands and ran down our wrists as we ate the ripe fruit. We licked our fingers. Thanh laughed.

"This celebrates my first day without pain," she said.

Cuổng invited me to watch Thanh walk. Taking her good hand, he pulled her to a sitting position, then lifted her legs off the bed. She steadied herself against his shoulder before she stood on her own. Holding on to the side rail, she edged along the bed and paused before she turned toward the nurses' station at the center of the long row of cots. The nurses looked up and spoke to her in Malay. Other patients raised themselves up on their elbows and called out to Thanh, who kept her eyes on her feet.

Listing like a boat overburdened on the port side, Thanh stepped with her left foot, swung her right and stepped again with her left. She turned when she reached the nurses' station, making a large arc like a ship changing course. A patient with her leg in traction commented in Chinese.

The child watched her left foot, then her right as she. stepped with the one and drew the other forward. She passed one bed and a second and a third, rocking as she walked. She passed a fourth bed and its patient spoke to her in Hindi. Only when Thanh reached Cuổng and me did she look up. Her face, gold with a spot of yellow, was radiant.

Some weeks later there was a Sunday afternoon pause on the island, perhaps an hour without interruptions. I wrote letters as I listened to Vietnamese folk songs I'd recorded at the Bidong radio station, which fed the loudspeakers.

Cường stopped by my room to say good-bye. He was on the departure list for Italy and had returned to Bidong to collect his things. He shuffled his feet as he stood near the row of snapshots over my desk. Removing his glasses with their cracked lens, he slowly polished them, then pulled on each of his fingers until the knuckle cracked.

"I told you a lie," he said.

"How's that?"

"I'm not Thanh's cousin after all. Just a friend of the family."

"It was a white lie," I said.

"I'm a single man," he added. "I have no family."

Cường told how Thanh's brothers had requested he escort the child to Trengganu because he could speak English. Her father had died in 1975 and her mother had remained in Saigon when the brothers and their two pre-teen sisters left. The brothers had fabricated Cường's family relationship because they feared I would think it unseemly for a strange man to care for a young girl.

I took down from the wall a snapshot of my valley farm. In the photograph a winter sunset tempered the snow into faint rust. A solitary figure climbed through the pasture toward a ridgetop, the house a red-roofed speck in the expanse of white behind her. Printing my address on the back, I wrote a Vietnamese farewell message wishing Cường joy and prosperity in his new life. Using language customary between equals, I wrote "older brother" in the salutation and "older sister" in the signature.

Cường was transferred to the Kuala Lumpur camp with the Scandinavian trailers housing the handicapped from Bidong. "I live here full of missing," he wrote. We lost touch after he left for Italy. A year later he found the snapshot, which he'd misplaced. "I have got married already with one

Italian girl," he wrote on a Christmas card. "Now I have one daughter with the name, Kiều GiaDa Maria Loan."

A month after Cương's departure, I returned to Trengganu to help with Thanh's early resettlement to the States so that she could begin extensive reconstructive surgery. At the hotel where oil developers and refugee workers stayed, I met with Neville, an Australian Red Cross doctor new to the MRCS team, and with two members of the American delegation. Neville had come out from the island to write the medical report needed for Thanh, and I'd invited the Americans in hopes they'd push the papers through faster.

As Neville pulled an examining screen around the child's bed, I asked whether she minded if the American women stayed. I hadn't seen Thanh's legs since she was burned because she always wore a sarong. She had full-skin burns with scars all down her right buttock, thigh and calf; on her left leg were deep keloid scars where surgeons had removed skin for grafting.

She reminded me of a twelve-year-old boy I'd seen ten years before at the German hospital ship in Đànẵng. The fingers of his left hand were soldered to his wrist, and his face was red scar tissue. He had one eye, two holes where his nose had been, and his mouth twisted to one side. He stopped me when he heard I'd come from his ancestral home, Quảng Ngãi, where he'd been napalmed. Thanh's right hand curled into a claw like that boy's in Đànẵng. With that hand, she gestured toward chairs, inviting the Americans to sit.

After visiting Thanh, we returned to the hotel for supper. I liked those Americans, Debbie and Sue, both idealistic Peace Corps returnees, both looking like southern Californians, though one came from New York. They said they would push Thanh's papers through as quickly as possible. And they did.

Three weeks later and three months after Thanh had fallen down the well in Zone F, her family's name was on the movement list to the States.

In the spring of 1980, Thanh and her sister and five brothers moved to Grand Blanc, Michigan, where they were sponsored by the town's churches. When I visited them two and a half years later, Thanh had begun to use her right hand after numerous operations. By then she was a high school freshman and, though frustrated by language difficulty in history and English, had earned straight A's. Her oldest brother was a maintenance worker in a nearby apartment complex, the second assembled electronic components in a California factory, and the third was studying electrical engineering at the local community college. Thanh's sister and two youngest brothers attended high school with her. They lived in an old farmhouse owned by the town of Grand Blanc, where they were the only Vietnamese.

Each year when I visit in the fall, Thanh and her brothers and sister wear blue jeans, T-shirts, and flip-flops. They prepare rice and egg rolls dipped in fish sauce, and for dessert Thanh passes around trick-or-treat candy. We share Bidong stories and news from Italy of Cuống and from San Diego of Hai. Each visit we watch football and they teach me a little more about the game. The teenagers work at their studies, having mastered the ability to do anything with the television on. At some point Thanh will ask if they seem like Americans yet; and at some point we'll turn off the TV and listen to Vietnamese music, choosing the most plaintive melodies as we remind each other how deeply we miss Bidong and how we long for Vietnam.

12
Rats

Once, on Bidong during the deep of the night, I awoke to find a rat in bed with me. I jerked at the scratch of its tiny claws scampering across my stomach. Swinging, I struck plumpness and soft fur. There was a thud against the back wall followed by a thrashing sound on the floor. In the morning, I brushed droppings from my pillow.

Usually first thing in the morning I'd go to the corner where I kept a bucket and dipper, and I'd splash my face with water. Once, while still foggy with sleep, I reached for the dipper, then shrieked. There, perched on its handle like the skipper on a doomed craft, was a wet rat. It didn't move; I couldn't tell whether it was dead or alive.

When I nudged the dipper, the rat slipped off and its whiskers brushed my wrist. It swam in circles, feet paddling, nose twitching as it bumped into the sides of the bucket. It clawed frantically at the red plastic side until I collected it in the dipper. When I held the container against the window, the rat scrambled out and stood motionless on the sill. Drops splashed off its yellow belly and collected in puddles around its feet. I tweaked the tail, which felt like nylon cord, and the rat ran off. Then I dipped water from the bucket and washed my face.

I'm a private person used to lots of physical and psychological space. Life on the island clawed at me, but at some point late each night I was at least able to close my door. The rats, however, cared nothing for doors. They ran in and out the windows and, if I closed the windows, they chewed holes in the floor. Their all-night gnawing sounded like fingernails scraping across wood. And they were persistent. A missile hurled in their direction sent them scurrying, but in a minute or two they'd return to gnaw once more. They ate everything: my soap, dictionaries, clothes, shoes, briefcase. Although, like all the islanders, I came to accept their destructiveness, I could never stop shivering at the feel of rats in my bed.

We always had a rat campaign going. After repeated requests for wooden snap traps, the mainland office sent fifty metal cages. Following several catches, these traps smelled of dead rat, an odor which warned off the live ones. The islanders scrubbed the traps in the surf because fresh water was strictly rationed. By the next use, the traps' metal doors had rusted so that the rats scampered in and then out with the bait. Soon the trappers returned to homemade snares, killing 14,296 rats during one of the Sanitation Division's ten-day campaigns. First prize went to two boys, who killed 237.

In the beginning of March, Dr. Lim Boo Liat, a World Health Organization specialist in rodent control, came to study rats on the island. Kuala Lumpur officials had insisted they needed Dr. Lim's written report before they could order the snap traps requested months earlier, yet because of the rats, these same officials refused to stay on the island overnight.

The MRCS staff called Dr. Lim "Ratman," a name which we used freely to his face, and one which I suspect he'd heard before. Of the many experts who visited Bidong during my stay, Ratman was the most perceptive and resourceful and one of the few to spend the night. A stocky Chinese man with a broad face and slightly waving hair, he was the only visitor to take himself on a tour of the island, speaking Chinese with whoever could respond. Within three hours of his arrival, he'd covered the seven residential zones, talked with Tho and myself about medical statistics, and with the Vietnamese Camp Committee about his study.

According to Dr. Lim, rats breed six to eight times per year. Each time they breed, the female bears four to eight offspring. Thus, after one year, a pair of rats—one male and one female—can generate a progeny totaling two thousand.

"It's not difficult to control this fecundity," Dr. Lim said in English as he helped himself to green beans in the Coconut Inn, "if you create a use for rats."

Lim looked up at Flower, who stood holding her white duck, which had just nipped Ratman's calf. At night the duck protected our food by snapping at the rats; during the day he chased off strangers without discriminating between intruders and visitors.

"Let's see if Flower will assist in controlling the rats," Lim said.

Instructing Flower in her native Chinese dialect, he made chopping motions with his hands, then with chopsticks flipped a green bean in his rice bowl as if sautéing meat in a wok. Flower's soft face contorted with disgust as she shook her head. Then she noticed Lim's merriment and laughed, her face tilting toward one shoulder.

"Ah, but really," Lim said in English, "rat is very tasty. It's rather like roast—" He stroked the soft white belly of Flower's pet. "Let's say it's rather like roast chicken."

Dr. Lim set up his laboratory in the Camp Committee office, where the Sanitation Division had built a wire cage the size of a grocery carton. Inside scrabbled several hundred rats caught the night before. Their claws scraped against the wire and their squeals were shrill.

"See if you can catch just one," Ratman said to the Vietnamese lab assistant, "without liberating the others!"

The assistant pulled a glove onto his hand. Jaw clenched, he reached tentatively into the cage that was a squirming mass of sleek fur. He grabbed a rat by the neck. It clawed at him as he stuffed it into a cloth sack to which he added a cotton ball soaked in chloroform.

Minutes later, Dr. Lim weighed the dead rat and laid it on a table. The inevitable crowd of onlookers watched as he carefully measured its body, tail, a hind foot, and an ear. With tweezers he picked mites out of the ear and dropped them into a test tube. He would check them later for scrub typhus. He recorded the species and sex.

"Mạnh quá.—How powerful," the spectators said when Lim examined the testicles, which bulged like tumors.

He slit the belly, snipped out the heart and dabbed it onto blotter paper. He would also use this blood sample later in tests for scrub typhus. He discarded the rat and took another from the white cloth sack. Once again he meticulously collected his data and since this specimen was female, recorded the number of fetus sacks—eight—swelling in her uterus.

"Haven't you a family-planning program, Dr. Thọ?" Ratman asked. Thọ laughed behind his hand.

According to Lim, there were three species of rats on

Bidong. Roughly 90 percent were common house rats identifiable by their yellow bellies and by tails longer than their bodies. These long tails provided balance and enabled house rats to run straight up the huts' cardboard walls. Since this same species existed in both Saigon and Trengganu, it was impossible to tell whether the rats had arrived on Vietnamese refugee boats, on Malaysian supply craft, or on both. Although Bidong house rats were the same length as their Saigon/Trengganu kin, they weighed twice as much.

"Their major problem," Dr. Lim said as he slit another rat's belly and pointed to fatty tissue surrounding its heart, "is obesity-related heart disease."

Another 8 percent of the rats were indigenous to Bidong. Lim identified them by their white bellies and tails shorter than their bodies. The other 2 percent were seaport rats, *rattus novegicus*, named so because of their migration on Norwegian boats some ten centuries before. The seaport rats had much longer bodies than house and field rats. Because their tails were far shorter than their bodies, they couldn't climb and were therefore ground rats.

The few scars on Bidong rats indicated that they fought little. "From this," Dr. Lim said, raising an eyebrow, "I conclude that food is plentiful." Thọ and I laughed, for the camp paths were strewn with garbage.

Dr. Lim checked each rat for fleas and placed samples in a test tube. Fleas were a major health concern on Bidong because they could carry bubonic plague.

Bubonic-plague bacilli cause blockage in the stomach of an infected flea so that it regurgitates, depositing the bacilli into each bite, thereby afflicting the host. Healthy fleas bite the diseased host, picking up the bacilli, which they quickly carry to other hosts, infecting them. For this reason, any unexplained increase in dead rats would have been cause for alarm, for once bubonic plague has significantly reduced the rat population, the plague-carrying fleas bite humans.

"Plague is endemic to Vietnam," Ratman said, looking at me. He dropped a flea into a test tube.

"I remember," I said.

During the war, Quảng Ngãi had had a significantly high incidence of the disease. The cases had filled an entire hospital ward. Once one of the Day Care Center children had caught plague. The lymph nodes in his groin swelled until they looked like black hard-boiled eggs. I could still remember the feel of his arms burning mine as I carried him into that plague ward, which was filled with the sour odor of black vomit. During the weeks when his darkened nodes threatened to burst, several other patients left the ward on stretchers for the morgue. But gradually the egglike buboes receded until his fever broke and the child went home, limp.

"You know it just takes one flea," Ratman said casually as he searched through the specimen's fur.

"No room for fleas on boat people boats," Thọ said. "They're too crowded."

Thọ knew better than anyone that Bidong was a volcano of people and rubbish and rats and that one plague-infected flea could spark an epidemic. He worked tirelessly on a camp-wide immunization program, but although we vaccinated against typhoid, diphtheria, tetanus, whooping cough, and polio, we had no access to vaccines against the rat-vectored diseases of typhus and plague.

Lim found only a few fleas in his examination. He concluded that most of them had jumped off during the rats' scrambling in the wire cage, but added that the rats' skin and fur indicated a low flea incidence.

"You escape," he said as he wrapped his calipers in a soft cloth and deposited them in his satchel. "Your rats are a nuisance, for the moment." He recommended we order simple wooden snap traps.

"Excellent idea!" Thọ said, winking at Lim. "Perhaps you forward this assessment to officials in Kuala Lumpur? In writing?"

At the beginning of May, two months after Ratman's visit and following numerous phone calls made whenever I was on the mainland, the Kuala Lumpur office agreed to send wooden snap traps.

It had grown so hot by then that I removed and hung over my desk a necklace fashioned from beads and nuts and a slim stone carved into the shape of a dove. That night a rat swung on the pendant until the thread broke and he landed with a thump. That same night the rats nibbled the calluses on my toes. They also ravaged a shipment of drugs temporarily stored in my room.

In the morning I swept up the scattered beads left from the necklace and placed them with the dove in a small box. The rats had eaten the nuts. I also swept up the multicolored capsules scattered like candy on the rough lumber floor and discarded them in a plastic bag. Gingerly I picked up four dead rats by their cordlike tails and dropped them into the sack. Each one landed with a plop, its soft yellow belly bloated on top of the invitingly decorated pharmaceuticals.

Chú bắt cái con chuột đó đi.
Ba bắt cái con chuột đó đi.

A dozen times a day that chorus pulsed over the loudspeakers with martial verve as if to draw troops to battle. Through-

out the camp, adults and particularly children picked up its
spicy tune and, clapping their hands, sang along:

Uncle, catch that rat, do.
Father, catch that rat, do.

As dark settled, children spread out over the camp's twisting paths. Some carried sticks and stones. Others set traps
they'd made from twigs and snippets of twine.

Catch 'em fast!
Step on 'em fast!
Kill the cunning rats! *Hu!*

The campaign went on for a week. Every night the children fanned out in search of rats and every morning they
brought their prey to the Sanitation Division to be counted.
By the end of one week, 11,093 rats had been cremated on
the orange mountainside above the camp. This time first
prize for the greatest catch went to a ten-year-old girl, who'd
apprehended 483.

"They're here!" Uncle called excitedly from the jetty one
morning in the middle of June, three and a half months after
Ratman's visit. "Come on, let's try one out."

We went into his sultry warehouse stacked to the ceiling
with pack rations. Uncle pulled open a carton and removed a
wooden snap trap, which he set. Immediately one of the two
staples holding the snap to the wood popped loose. He tried a
second trap and its staple also broke.

"Ah ha!" he said in his lilting Indian voice when a third
trap's staple held. Carefully he placed the trap on the sand
floor of the warehouse. From one of the ration packets he

removed a small bag of rice about the size of a rat and, squatting, gently rolled it onto the trap. The trap snapped, ensnaring the rice but when Uncle removed the bag, he discovered the snap had broken.

"Rats!" he said, hurling the trap back into its carton.

⊛ 13
Roofsitter

One evening, after I'd been on the island four months, I was going over boat lists in the Camp Committee office when Jim came to fetch me. A patient had climbed onto the hospital roof and refused to come down.

I slipped my pencil behind my ear and went out into the oppressively humid air that had hovered over the camp for days. Jim's back, moving ahead of me down the winding path, signaled urgency, weariness and distress. "I don't need this on top of everything else," seemed to be the message.

The sun was sinking into the sea when we arrived; the beach was solid spectators, faces tilting upward, voices excited. Malaysian guards tried to disperse onlookers with sticks and rifle butts, only to have a larger crowd coalesce.

In front of the hospital I kicked off my flip-flops and climbed the new water tower the Engineering Division had built. From the tower I scrambled onto the roof. Its height was greater than my roof at home but the pitch was less frightening. Keeping my weight low and spread out, I skittered like a sand crab over the asbestos sheeting.

A young man crouched near the ridgepole. Two male nurses squatting a few feet away were trying to persuade him to climb down, but he gritted his teeth and shook his head. His nose and eyebrows, sharp for an Oriental, quivered. His eyes were wild, yet they had a calculating tint that made me think he'd chosen to climb the rafters at just that hour in the evening when the sea drew everyone to her edge. A few days before, the Swiss had taken a large number of people with mental-health problems. We'd been anticipating an upsurge of distress from those who hoped illness might facilitate their early departure.

I would have stayed there quietly with that young man until I felt comfortable leaving him by himself, if I'd had my choice. At home I liked nothing better in the fall than to climb with a bucket of patching tar up onto the roof and listen to the elm leaves rustling before they floated downward.

In Quảng Ngãi, there had been a roof I often escaped to. There, in the afternoon, I gazed at pony carts creaking down the main street. At dusk the roof shook as tanks retreated from the airport to the American compound for the night; by evening there was the rumble of American helicopters and the splattering rattle of their red-arced bullets, as abstract to me on that rooftop as a slash of red paint across a modern canvas.

Now, on the Bidong hospital roof, I felt as if I'd discovered a sanctuary. The horizon was a crimson backdrop to *Red Crescent 2* bobbing at the end of the jetty. The sea breathed shades of green and purple; the voices of spectators on the beach seemed removed, as if filtered through sleep.

I studied the young man squatting near the lone palm that arched through a hole in the hospital roof. Sweat had collected on his angular nose and around his wild eyes. He licked his lips; I could hear his teeth grinding.

Suddenly there was a thumping sound. Turning around, I saw the silhouettes of Jim and Neville loom across the roof. Neville looked like a colonial explorer in his white hat, matching ivory shorts and shirt, and his strapped sandals.

Jim scrambled past Neville and crouched down in front of me. He ordered the young man off the roof at once. He told him that the Malaysian guards were insisting on immediate action. When I translated this, the young man shook his head so violently that his sweat sprinkled like sea spray. He ground his teeth mercilessly and refused to talk to us. Despite my protests, Jim and Neville decided to sedate him. Neville scurried back across the roof and down the water tower in search of a hypodermic needle.

The man's lips tightened and his teeth stopped grinding. Only his eyes moved, darting as if at any moment he might break away, tear past the palm that arched through the rooftop and plunge into the crowd looking up from below. The nurses edged closer. I poked my arm through the ridge vent and, hooking my left elbow around the ridgepole, spread my weight over the roof. With my right arm I reached toward the young man's shoulder. Neville climbed back onto the roof. With the hypodermic poised, he towered over the cowering figure.

The man bolted.

Vietnamese nurses snatched his wrists and ankles. I hooked his neck. Neville lunged, his foot smashing into the roof. He lurched: a crash like metal shattering.

We froze, hearts pounding. The young man pinned to the roof was gasping. We were all gasping as we peered down through the jagged hole and into the men's ward far below. The ward was empty. Cots covered with blue-striped plastic looked like furnishings in a doll's house. Asbestos splinters cluttered the floor. From the doorway, patients stared up at Neville, who stared back down at them through the hole at his feet.

While we restrained the young man, Neville searched for a vein. He shot the injection, loaded, and shot again. In a minute the young man's wild eyes drooped and in two or three minutes his teeth ceased grinding. Jim called down through the hole for sheeting. We rolled the limp form onto blue plastic and slid it along the ridgepole. Once past the palm, we crossed to a lower roof and down into the hospital ward carpeted with asbestos splinters.

When I spoke with the roofsitter the next morning, we quickly switched from Vietnamese to English, which he'd learned from listening to the radio. He'd never conversed with a native speaker before, yet his usage and accent were impeccable.

"It's fearful," the male nurses said of his language ability.

"I think you knew what you were doing up on that roof," I said to Roofsitter, guessing that he perceived the manipulative effect of his actions.

"I think you may be correct," he said, slowly licking his lips. The day before had been the year anniversary of his leaving Vietnam, yet no country had accepted him. He couldn't tolerate the crowds on the island and, longing for solitude, had often escaped for days alone in the jungle on the far side of Bidong Mountain.

Coincidentally, four days later Roofsitter's name appeared on a departure list for the United States. However, the following morning he refused to join that movement just as it was leaving.

"I want to go to China," he said as we stood in the hospital foyer.

"China! But we don't have any contact with Communist countries," I said.

"My grandparents live in Canton. I'm Chinese and Canton's my *quê hương*—my ancestral home."

"But you applied for America. You've been accepted!"

"I want to go to China."

I fetched Jim. He strode into the foyer and stood towering over the young man. Women with squalling babies turned away from the outpatient clinic and pressed toward them.

"You mean you're refusing to go to America!" Jim shouted.

Roofsitter licked his lips. "Not exact—"

"You mean you're refusing to go, is that what you mean? You mean you're refusing to get on that boat and go!" Jim pointed his pipe stem toward *Black Gold* waiting at the end of the jetty. His words were diamond sharp.

"No, no, not exac—"

"Then you get your things, young man, and you get them darn quick!" Jim waved his pipe toward the men's ward and stomped out. Roofsitter pushed through the crowd of staring patients, who turned back toward the clinic door.

"Look," I said in the men's ward as he collected his extra shirt, toothbrush, and comb, "you think Bidong's crowded, but wait till you get to Kuala Lumpur. That camp's a prison. If you act crazy just once, they'll ship you to Gohore lunatic asylum for the rest of your life. And that's the truth."

Outside the ward window, the megaphone stopped rasping names on the movement list; the last departing family straggled down the jetty.

"You'd better hurry," I said. "I'll get you a book, and you keep your nose tethered to it. Do you understand?" Roofsitter nodded.

If on Bidong fresh food was treasure, then books were bounty. Paul, the British engineer, gave me his three spy novels. With these I ran down the jetty. The captain threw *Black Gold*'s engines into reverse. He leaned out the forecastle window.

"Maybe we leave at ten o'clock," he yelled at me, "maybe we leave at eleven!"

Roofsitter was leaning over the railing, a smile dominating his angular features. Jim had assigned him two orphan boys to tend during the trip. I passed Roofsitter the books, and we clasped hands just before *Black Gold* parted from the mooring barge.

Some weeks later I heard Roofsitter was having a rough time in the Kuala Lumpur transit camp, but after that I heard no more news of him. However, a month after that report, I attended a meeting where UN staff presented Bidong resettlement figures accumulated from the first departures in 1979, through to May 1980:

United States	27,747
Canada	7,337
Australia	6,400
France	1,640
W. Germany	1,580
Switzerland	899
Holland	735
Italy	565

and so on down the list of twenty-four countries until the very last entry:

China	1

❂ 14
All Alone, Ma!

*I'm in the Quảng Ngãi prison. Designed by French colo-
nialists for four hundred, it confines fourteen hundred Communist suspects. I've come to interpret for the Quaker doctor
during his weekly medical visit.*

*"Afraid," a young woman says. She cracks her knuckles
one by one. Her hands are rough and her nails are short and
broken. She's recently had convulsions. As the doctor assem-
bles his otoscope, I explain that it's like a flashlight.*

*"Afraid," she says. When she whimpers, the doctor re-
places the otoscope in his black bag. She begins to cry. Then
she starts to sob and beat her arms against the cot. She strikes
her head into its frame.*

"Thôi! Thôi!—Enough! Enough!" she yells, kicking.

*Sitting on the cot, I grab her wrists while another prisoner
clamps her ankles. The doctor leaves to fetch a sedative.*

*The woman jerks and moans, throwing herself back and
forth, knocking her skull against the bed frame with a sound
like a dull ax against wood. Quickly I scoot around on the*

cot, throwing my legs over her so that they surround her torso. Her head slaps against my thighs. Holding her wrists, I lean over her. The muscles down my back and legs stretch as she rips me from one side to the other, pulling my arms tight over her breasts then shrieking and hurling me away. Her mouth contorts with terror. Perspiration seeps from her body as she twists. Sweat runs down my forehead and cheeks; it slips off my chin and drops onto her twisted face.

"Thôi!—Enough!" She screams, her eyes widening in horror as sheer as razors. Grimacing, she twists, throwing me and the prisoner holding her feet off balance.

"Thôi. Thôi," we each say softly.

"Thôi!" she shrieks, letting forth a scream that slices our ears.

The doctor appears with the sedative and we lean into her, pressing even more into her wild thrashing while he swabs a vein and inserts the needle, releasing the plunger. She screams and yells and rolls about, kicking the man at her feet, knocking her head against my thighs, yanking my arms and shoulders hither and yon. Her eyes roll about and she sobs and cries and moans and finally, finally after whimpering like a beaten dog, finally she sleeps.

Later as the doctor and I are leaving, the prisoner who held her ankles speaks softly in Vietnamese. "She just came from down the street."

"The new building?" I say in a low voice. American Seabees have recently completed an interrogation center. It's surrounded by barbed wire coils and protected with corner watch towers like a World War II concentration camp. American officers enter it every morning as I'm driving children to the Day Care Center.

"Yes, the new building," the prisoner says, shuffling and

*looking around. No one is nearby. "They attached electrodes
to her nipples."*

On a cot in the Bidong general ward, a young woman
writhed, gauze strips binding her limbs to the bedstand.
"Má!" she cried. Coarse black hair fell over her eyes, which
were set wide apart under thick brows. Her plump cheeks
and full lips made her look like a young child, though I knew
she had to be in her mid-twenties.

Other women with toddlers on their hips pressed toward
the cot. "Look, look," they said to one another.

"Má! Chết, Má! Dead, Mother! *Đi! Đi!* Go! Everyone go!
Don't leave, *Má!"* The woman's childlike face dripped sweat.
Clenching her fists, she jerked against the restraints. She tore
at her trousers and ripped open her shirt.

A young man leaned over and resnapped her blouse. He
wore shorts and a faded orange shirt. With his narrow lips
and hair cut very short all over his head, he gave an impres-
sion of severity.

I sat on the young woman's cot and spoke in a voice I'd
often used whenever a disturbed child wailed on my school
bus.

The woman screamed and flailed, striking my shoulder.
"Má!" she shrieked. "Alone! Everyone go. *Đi! Đi!* Go, *Má!"*

I continued talking, my rhythms repetitive. I relied heavily
on *"mệt"*— "tired" and *"buồn"*—"sad," two Vietnamese ad-
jectives which, taken together, encompass the world's sor-
rows in a way similar to the soul term "blues."

"Her husband left her, and both her infant sons are dead,"
said the young man with the narrow lips. He told me his
name, Minh. The young woman's name, he said, was Mai.

"They've left me!" Mai shrieked, and her eyes rolled up
into her head.

"Terrifying," said an old man with a wispy beard. He stood at the edge of the onlookers.

Neville arranged for a sedative. Over the sound of Mai's grinding teeth I could hear him request sticking plaster. "Let her be," I told him grimly. I'd already had enough of his hypodermics. I turned back to talk to Mai, changing pronouns from "miss" to "little sister."

"No one left, *Má!*" Mai cried out. Shrieking, she ripped open her blouse. The snaps popped like rifle fire.

"It's all right, child," I said, changing pronouns again.

"They left me." Her screams were subsiding.

"It's all right, child."

She lay back, gasping, sweating. For the first time she looked up, and when she focused on my gaze, her brow furrowed. She grasped my hand and ran her fingers over mine. A smile flickered across her face.

"*Má,*" she said.

"It's all right, child." I stroked the hair at the edge of her brow. It was black and coarse and slick with sweat.

"All alone, *Má,*" she said. Her voice was slow and thick.

"It's all right, child."

Neville pushed through the gawkers. In his ivory shorts and shirt he towered over us, a hypodermic in his hand.

"She'll be okay," I said. "Let her be."

"This will help her." Tilting a small vial, he inserted the needle.

"Let her be, Neville. Let her—"

He gave the injection, and I was instantly furious with him. The woman broke loose from me, jerking and wailing and yelling, "*Ði! Ði!* Go! All go! Everyone go! Me alone!" She threw her arms out like splints and whenever she shouted, her eyes rolled up out of sight.

"Chết rồi.—Dead already," murmured an old woman among the spectators hanging over us like a humid cloud.

The young woman tossed, yanking at the gauze straps. Minh grabbed her wrists. He held them, restraining her as she thrashed and writhed, shrieking and moaning. Sweat poured from her face.

Minh pushed against her shoulders and I took her hands, but then she grabbed onto me. Clamping my wrists and digging her fingernails into my veins, she hurtled me against the plywood wall.

"All alone, *Má!*"

She lay back for a moment, but then she broke again, thrashing and moaning, *"Chết, Má!* Everyone go! Me alone!"

I felt a tap on my shoulder. It was Thúy Hằng, who was seven years old and took care of her great-grandmother. With both hands Thúy Hằng presented a bowl of water and a tin spoon. Tiny gold hoops swayed in her ears as she folded her arms across her chest and bowed. She looked up and smiled. New front teeth half filled the gap in her upper jaw.

I spooned the water into Mai's mouth. Her lips were crusty and her teeth were covered with scum. She licked her lips and looked at me with glazed eyes.

Thúy Hằng waited at the foot of the cot until I finished. She took the empty bowl, bowed and left. From down the hall came the sound of a dipper banging against a heavy cauldron. Inside the ward, rice bowls and tea mugs clattered as patients collected their utensils and shuffled out of the room. Soon the ward filled with the smell of cooked rice. Thúy Hằng brought more water and waited at the foot of the cot while I spooned it into Mai's mouth.

The late afternoon sun edged across the sky as Minh and I restrained, soothed and spooned water; restrained, soothed and spooned water. Finally, Mai lay back and slept, her eyes in shade.

I left the hospital and walked along the camp's main path, pushing through the steam of bodies. I had no destination.

"Hello, hello! Where do you go?" A little boy took my hand.

"For a walk," I said. "Where are you going?"

"For a walk."

The child led me through the sweating bodies; the greasy arms of others slipped against mine. We let go of each other's hand and pressed through the crowd and caught hands again. When we stopped at a stall, the vendor removed a croissant from a metal sheet she'd just pulled from an oil-drum oven. The aroma of warm bread advertised its freshness. The child and I split the croissant, peeling it layer by layer as we nibbled its crisp crust. The dough inside was warm, soft and slightly sweet. We continued along the path and paused at a stall where a man engraved dragons onto a metal plate.

When we reached Zone C beach, the child bowed and scampered off toward the surf. His footprints were distinct near my own before they turned and pointed toward the sea. Then they merged with the rush of footprints crossing, footprints in tandem, footprints jostling, big wide prints with indistinct toes, tiny little ones with prominent arches, the sharp tread of a new arrival's recently distributed flip-flop, the blurred shape of a long-term resident's worn sandal.

Voices, each with stories, seemed to rise from the myriad footprints. The voices swirled together, engulfing me like shimmering waves of heat, reverberating in my ears, resonating with the cry "Me alone! All alone!" At first I thought I was hearing an echo of Mai in the ward but then realized that the anguished voice was mine. I looked for the dark head of the child who'd led me to the beach, but he was indistinguishable from others bobbing in the surf. The children laughed and shouted in the breakers; I walked on, not knowing or caring where my feet led me.

Soon I came near a young man who was arranging tables and benches made of hull planks. One table top had a boat number stenciled on it. The man hummed along with the song that was playing on the cafe's tape recorder:

Hai mươi năm nội chiến từng ngày
Gia tài của mẹ để' lại cho con
Gia tài của mẹ là nước Việt buồn.

Twenty years of civil war
The mother's legacy she leaves for her child
The mother's legacy is a sad Vietnam.

From the cafe next door a Simon and Garfunkel tape answered:

Hello, darkness, my old friend
I've come to talk with you again
Because a vision softly creeping
Left its seeds while I was sleeping
And the vision that was planted in my brain
Still remains
Within the sounds of silence.

I left the beach and pushed my way back along the crowded path to the Coconut Inn, hoping that Flower would be there. I chose a seat across from a hole in the asbestos roof, where a coconut had landed a few days before. Removing my flip-flops, I twisted my toes in the sand. Flower's duck rubbed its soft feathers against my calves.

Flower brought two steaming glasses and sat next to me, taking my hand. "You're *buồn*—sad," she said. Her round face with its rosy cheeks tilted toward one shoulder. "Here, please drink this." She presented me with one of the glasses. Her brew—a concoction of red tea, instant coffee, and sweetened condensed milk—was warm and comforting.

The next morning Mai continued in fits of delirium, always a crowd around her. She needed isolation, but there was no privacy on Bidong; she required professional psychiatric care, but we had none.

After three days of delirium, she could say her name. It meant "Plum." When I asked for her boat number, Mai spoke each numeral slowly as if dredging through mud. I was sitting on the edge of her cot. I'd just come from English class and had with me *The Story of Ping,* a children's picture book classic sent to me by a friend in the States. I used it as a beginners' text.

"*Đẹp quá.*—So beautiful," Mai said, petting the duck on the book's cover. Slowly she turned the pages. From the colorful drawings she recounted the lost duckling's search for his mother, father, aunts, uncles, and forty-two cousins, who lived in a wise-eyed boat on the Yangtze River. As she spoke, her voice sounded thick. When she laughed, her eyes remained dull.

Within that week at least a dozen people stopped me, asking if they could leave the island early because of mental health problems. "I'm sorry," I said after each request, "the Swiss aren't taking any more mental health cases." This was true.

Within that same week two other young women were brought into the hospital, screaming and thrashing. The second woman complained of a fearful headache. For three days, the Vietnamese doctors gave her medicine while her family hovered, fretting. To relieve her pain, the woman's sisters pinched her upper chest and forehead until the skin purpled. They beseeched us to send her immediately to Switzerland.

"I'm sorry," I said. "The Swiss aren't taking any more people."

Following traditional Chinese medicine, the sisters removed the woman's blouse and rolled her onto her abdomen. They twisted ration papers into wads, laid them on her back and ignited them. Immediately they encased each blaze in an instant-coffee jar. These they removed after the flames had consumed all available oxygen. The jars made a popping sound as the vacuum seals broke away from red disks burned onto the skin.

Thọ noticed that the woman's thrashing increased whenever he approached. I noticed the same effect. Whenever we shooed the family members away, they'd return, fretful, begging for the woman's early departure from the island. They protested when we decided to transfer her to Trengganu.

"How shall we write this medical report?" I asked Thọ as I pulled together papers to accompany the patient.

"Let's recommend *no* medicine," he answered. "And *no* attention."

Ten hours after the patient arrived in Trengganu, I received radio news that she was sitting up and had written her family a three-page letter.

I asked Thọ to place an announcement on the loudspeakers:

BECAUSE THE SWISS DELEGATION HAS
OVERACCEPTED, IT WILL NOT RETURN

TO BIDONG. THEREFORE, MEDICAL
AND MENTAL HEALTH CASES CANNOT
LEAVE THE ISLAND EARLY.

I requested he run the announcement for a week.

That night when I stopped by Mai's room after English
class, she was brandishing a stick at Minh, who'd been taking
care of her. Dropping the stick, she charged him, her hands
clamping his throat. Then she saw me.

"I am mentally ill, *Má*, mentally ill," she yelled in English.
Yet when I spoke of possible resettlement in France, she
began to calm down and I could see she was struggling for
control.

Later, though, she paced in the downstairs hall. "*Chết,
Má,*" she called out. "All gone. *Đi! Đi!* Go! Everyone go!" She
paced, and she sang in a loud voice. Other patients got out of
their cots and stood in the dark hall, rubbing their eyes. I took
Mai by the shoulders and led her into the partially completed
new delivery room, which at that time was serving as her
isolation ward. After talking her down, I returned to bed, but
awakened shortly to the sound of her singing loudly, turbu-
lently, in the downstairs hall.

One morning several days later, Chris and I were the first
ones to breakfast in the Coconut Inn. We both stirred our tea,
although neither of us took sugar. We were waiting for Jim
Hart.

Chris, a New Zealand Red Cross nurse, had recently arrived on the island to work for six months. She was a robust
blond woman who spoke with a clipped accent. Neville
called her "Sister," following the formality used by Australian doctors. Some of the Vietnamese hospital staff, cheer-

fully confused, called her "Sister Christ." That name stuck among MRCS staff, who enjoyed its irony, for after a hard day's work Sister Christ liked nothing better than to kick off her shoes, sip a gin and tonic, and create merriment.

Chris had just learned that Jim was fed up with Mai's naked screaming in the hospital halls. He wanted to ship her to the Trengganu psychiatric ward on the next boat because he felt she took too much of our energy. Chris had worked in a psychiatric ward, and I had once directed an emergency mental health service in Ohio. We both felt Mai would go irreparably mad if she were isolated in a Malaysian asylum. Besides, we thought she retained some control.

Jim flopped his frumpy green hat on the table's rough boards and sat down. The foaming mug on his beer drinker's T-shirt rested gently on a rising pot belly. Chris gave him an insistent gaze as she proposed keeping Mai on the island.

"Absolutely not!" he barked. He banged a pitcher on the table, slopping tea onto his hat. "Wonderful," he said, shaking off the tea drops.

"Give her one more chance, Farty Hart," Chris said in her precise speech. "It's us she's bugging, not you."

"No," Jim said.

Chris stirred her tea. The spoon clinked against the glass.

"Give us one more chance with her," I said. Chris was glaring at Jim. He glanced back and forth at each of us, and when his attention settled uneasily on me, I knew Sister Chris had stared him down.

"Okay, okay!" He knocked the ashes out of his pipe and clenched the stem in his teeth. "But any of that singing and screaming, ripping off clothes, chasing the cooks with sticks, any more of that stuff just once and we poke her full of needles and ship her out on the next boat."

"Sure thing, Hearty Fart," Chris said.

In the hospital, Chris and I sat with Mai between us on her cot. Chris took one hand, I the other. While I spoke in Vietnamese, Chris looked her firmly in the eyes. Minh, the young man who tended Mai, stood nearby.

"Do you remember when Jim came in last night?" I asked. "How he pointed across the sea, how he held his fingers to his temples and then to the light switch? Do you remember the crackling noise he made?"

Mai nodded.

"And did you understand what he meant to say?"

Mai looked at Chris, then at me. Her gaze was swampy.

I laid out the choices. If she held her spells at bay, she might move early to France. If she let them return just once, she'd be shipped to a Malaysian asylum, where they'd attach electrodes to her forehead.

I repeated these choices. Minh, who'd been listening, repeated them. Thọ had joined us. Some days earlier, he'd written a short story about Mai. He, too, listened and repeated the choices. Chris reiterated them in English.

Mai looked at each of us, her shoulders drooping. From the hallway came voices layering over voices. Suddenly Mai raised her right hand in a fist with the thumb up. "It's gone, *Má!*" she said in English.

"But what if you decide to let it return?" I asked in Vietnamese.

"I don't move to France. But it's gone, *Má! Gone good!*" Both her thumbs jerked up.

We made arrangements. All of us, including Mai, agreed she'd fare better at home away from hospital crowds. Minh would bring her down each morning to see Chris and in the afternoon he'd return alone for Mai's special food rations. For now, she was to rest and then fetch me when she was ready to leave.

Some hours later, Bạch, who was the Vietnamese hospital manager, Chris, Thọ, and I were discussing how to spend eight hundred and thirty American dollars donated by the French embassy, when Mai wandered past the door. She was singing, *"Hò ho ho hó ho ho hò/Con ngủ đi con*—Ho ho ho ho ho ho ho/Go to sleep, my child."* Her voice was a gentle hum.

We looked at each other uneasily. "Where are you going?" Thọ called out in Vietnamese.

"Visiting."

"Then come in and visit here." Thọ made a space between us on the bench, and Mai sat down. As we continued our discussion, she slowly drew her finger down a stripe on my sleeve. Speck by speck she removed the lint. Carefully she arranged the cuff.

"Let's ask for a washing machine?!" Bạch suggested.

"Brilliant!" Chris said. "For the sheets they'll buy to replace the blue-striped plastic!"

"Good!" Mai said. She clapped her hands and jerked her thumbs upright. "Gone good?"

When we'd finished meeting, Mai led Minh and me down the hospital steps to the central path. Carrying a small bundle, she walked into the streaming crowd. Always a step ahead, she led us deep into Zone C. We wound our way around huts and stepped over open sewers that reeked. The air smelled of smoke from cooking fires. People eating their rice stared at us.

"Where are you going?" an old woman squatting inside a hut asked. Holding a bowl just below her chin, she shoveled rice into her mouth with chopsticks.

"Home," Mai answered.

She took another turn, then another, and we stepped into a

hut. A ladder led to a board sleeping loft used by the hut's ten residents. The sand floor was etched with footprints.

"Too crowded," Mai said as she set her bundle on the sand.

The next day I spoke with a visiting official about Mai. He was a tall man with a ginger mustache, who had been appointed by the French President to investigate refugee conditions. His name was Michel, and from the beginning I liked the look of him. His wife, who was Saigonese, had remained in Paris. Since Michel's English was as weak as my French, we communicated in Vietnamese. He agreed to telex the French ambassador, whom he knew personally, requesting that Mai and her friend Minh be accepted for the next day's movement to France.

After the telex was drafted, Michel and I climbed to the radio shack perched atop Religious Hill. Soon after I started the transmission, spelling out each word, the connection with the UN Trengganu office faltered. With each repetition the radio battery waned. I shouted as if will power alone could hurl words eighteen miles across the sea:

. . . WHEN HER FIRST CHILD DIED FROM FEVER OF UNKNOWN ORIGIN, SHE ENTERED A MENTAL HOSPITAL. UPON DISCHARGE THREE MONTHS LATER, HER HUSBAND LEFT HER. SHE LIVED ALONE WITH HER SECOND SON. EIGHT MONTHS LATER SHE LEFT IN SEARCH OF LIBERTY, BUT FAILED AND RETURNED. HER SECOND SON WAS SO TIRED HE GOT SICK AND DIED. THEN SHE CAME TO BIDONG . . .

Later that afternoon Michel appeared with a telex from the ambassador, who had granted Mai and Minh permission to leave the next morning for France. I paged Mai on the loudspeakers.

"I am full of missing, *Má,*" she said.

That evening I took the UN launch to Trengganu to run errands. The next morning I stopped by the mainland jetty to see Mai and Minh, who were coming from Bidong with departees for France.

As soon as *Black Gold* landed, Mai was standing next to me, saying the traditional farewells but using "child" for "I" and *"Má"* for "you." Minh stood behind her. Then they walked down the jetty, each carrying a small bundle like a child's bookbag. They picked up their lunch of bread, eggs, and tea, and climbed onto a bus.

A week later, I heard that they'd left for France; after that, I heard nothing more.

🌀 15
The Riot

One morning an oil supply ship arrived with 352 new refugees and 2 corpses. A total of 28 passengers had died en route. The landing barge was a chaos of humanity: people picking up small children, people fainting, empty stretchers arriving, filled ones leaving. Patients occupied every hospital cot, sometimes two or three to each. All morning and afternoon I bathed toddlers and sponged the faces of children, young women and old men. I spooned water into mouths. The lips were bloated and chapped, the cheeks were dark and cracking. The eyes stared.

On the floor of the children's ward, toddlers curled inside their mothers' arms. One woman, whose husband had been among the twenty-eight, held a naked baby to her breast. Over each of her thighs climbed a naked toddler. Purple bubbles crusted the children's bodies. The mother shifted her baby from one breast to the other. During the trip she'd collected her toddlers' urine and drunk it in order to nurse the infant.

By evening the dead were buried and the living settled.

Nine men, who'd been accused of killing the twenty-eight, were safely confined inside the barbed-wire-encircled guards' compound. Several passengers had pointed at the nine men. *"Việt-cộng*—Vietnamese Communist," they said. Others called the men gangsters. Some—and they were the ones I tended to believe—said that during the trip there'd been frightening brawls over sips of water.

Whatever happened, it was clear from the crowd rumbling all day outside the compound that the lives of the nine men inside were endangered. All thirteen thousand Bidong residents had chosen to leave Vietnam because of dissatisfaction with the new regime. The accusation "Communist," even if randomly spoken, could inflame the entire community.

It was 3 A.M. when I turned in. All that night I lay awake because of wails coming from the children's ward. The mothers, their eyes oozing pus, paced with screaming babies at their breasts. The babies were covered with erupting rashes; they would not be comforted. In the next ward, five other children from two orphaned families slept, three in one bed, two in another.

The early morning voices coming from outside the guards' compound were like a watchdog's first growl. Daylight was still a haze. I was dozing when the door latch turned and someone padded into my room. I opened my eyes to see one of the orphaned children peering down at me. He wanted to know if he could leave that morning for America.

At midday, Tú, a fourteen-year-old whose father had died on the boat, gave me two diamond rings and a pair of jade earrings for safekeeping. Her tongue was enlarged like a mongoloid's and her dull gaze reminded me of children on my school bus. She handed me a twenty-dollar greenback she'd brought from Vietnam. I changed this into Malaysian ringgit, which I agreed to keep for her and dispense as weekly spending money. Vũ and Khanh watched. Ages twelve and ten, they were Tú's brothers. The skin peeling in the shape of a mask around Vũ's eyes made him look like a raccoon. Someone had given Khanh a man's pajama shirt, which dwarfed him.

In the afternoon I took Tú, Vũ, and Khanh to buy flip-flops at one of the vendors' stalls. As we walked down the main path, holding hands four abreast, Vũ and Khanh strode as if recovered, but Tú dragged, dazed. Her tongue remained swollen, with white spots.

All day long a mob pulsed outside the barbed wire encircling the guards' compound. Inside cowered the nine men accused of killing the twenty-eight. Whenever one of the nine appeared in view, the crowd raised fists and shouted. Even at the hospital, I could hear the rumbling.

Leaning out from her hut, a woman stopped me that afternoon as I was crossing the main sewer. Her son, Kim, was the island's only blond child. I'd met the mother some weeks before, when she'd brought Kim into the hospital after other children had beaten his head with sticks.

Once again she was in tears. She pointed to some boys playing in a massive gray boat wrecked at the exit of the sewer. "These children call me filthy! They call me animal! They call me filthy because I married an American, have an American child. I'm a good mother. Ask my son if I don't care for him!"

Through a window in the hut's blue plastic, I could see Kim squatting like any other Bidong child on the floor. He held a rice bowl close to his mouth and scraped it clean with chopsticks. His hair, bleached almost white from playing in the surf, hung down over his eyes. He did not look up.

"I have an American husband!" the woman said, pulling a

handkerchief from her shirt pocket. She unwrapped it to show an envelope.

"There he is!" she said. "See! A good American husband! I go to him in Cali."

"Do you know where in California he lives?" I asked.

She pointed to the envelope. Of the water-smudged return address I could only just make out "LA, Ca." The postmark was February 19, 1975. Her husband's name was Thomas Smith. She wanted me to help her find him.

"Los Angeles is as big as Saigon," I said. "People move a lot and Smith is as common a name as Nguyễn. It will be very hard."

"*Mỹ! Mỹ!*—American! American!" Boys with straight black hair wet from swimming chanted as they passed us. They pointed through the hut window at Kim and jeered. I left saddened, imagining the taunts California children would hurl at him.

That evening Uncle invited me to supper at the home of the friends we'd visited the first day of Tết. It had been five months since I'd seen that Chinese-Vietnamese family: the grandmother with her beautiful black teeth, the gold-toothed parents, and their twelve children. Since we'd met, the father had learned English and I'd improved my Vietnamese. Over supper of rice and noodles he asked if I were Buddhist.

"Maybe a little," I said. "Mostly I'm Quaker."

"And that is what?" he asked.

I explained the Quakers' belief that the Holy Spirit is equally present in every person regardless of sex, race, color, religion, or political beliefs. It followed, I said, that killing another person was the same as extinguishing the Spirit, and for this reason Quakers often refused to fight in wars. I mentioned that most Quakers didn't feel the need for a priest or minister because they believed all were equal before the Spirit. Thus, their services were usually silent worship without clergy or ritual.

"Maybe is like our Buddhist a little," the father said, nodding, the tip of his gold tooth catching the frail kerosene light.

It was Sunday, midday. As I left the hospital to check on new arrivals, I noticed people running toward the guards' compound, people running down all the snaking lanes that fed into the main path. I ran, too, following the crowd toward the beach. There, Malaysian guards were escorting the nine prisoners. Frightened by the crowds rumbling outside their compound, the guards had decided to transfer the suspects to Trengganu for safekeeping. *Black Gold*, her engines running, was waiting for them at the end of the jetty.

On the beach there were men everywhere. Running, yelling. Fists flailing. They yanked the prisoners into the sea, beat them, kicked them. I stood on the beach, paralyzed with fear. Although I can swim, even in a wading pool with toddlers I'll cringe at the slightest splashing. But more men were racing past me, pouring into the sea; there was nothing to do but follow.

I dashed to the group farthest out. Water swirled above my waist, everyone splashing, flailing, the victim moaning. The men pushed the prisoner under the water and held him there while they beat, beat. Grabbing at arms, I elbowed the assailants aside and yanked the man from the sea bottom. I shook him.

"*Chết rồi*," he gasped.

Blood dribbled from his head onto my shirt. We were standing in water above our waists and he was gasping and I was gasping and swinging my arms to keep away the men who darted at us. I dragged the bloodied man to the beach where I stood holding him up while the mob seethed around us. I asked a nurse I knew from the hospital to fetch a stretcher, but he only stared with hate at the injured man, who collapsed on the sand. Rumbling, the mob edged closer. Just when I feared I could no longer restrain the crowd, Jim was there, scooping the man onto his shoulder. Glancing at the mass of men who blocked his way to the boat, he ran with the injured man back toward the guards' compound. From the beach I chose a pair of flip-flops and left to fetch Neville.

In the compound, Jim and Neville discussed carrying the man with the bloody head out to the boat on a stretcher. He lay on the ground, his right cheek swollen like mumps. Blood dribbled from his forehead. Another man whom Jim had pulled from the water started to cry when I asked where he felt pain. Both men said they weren't Communists, only students. The other prisoners hid behind a water tank. Outside the barbed wire raged an angry mob.

Near the compound gate two young women sobbed. They said their father, who was huddling behind the water tank, wasn't a Communist. One of the sisters told me that when she'd fainted during the trip, collapsing into the rising bilge water, a man moved over into the space she'd vacated. Her father hauled her up from the bilge, but just when he did so, elbowing to regain her lost place, the young man who'd taken it went delirious with thirst. Screaming, he threw himself into the sea.

Inside the guards' compound, the Malaysian commander was talking to Jim and Neville, advising them to wait for things to quiet.

"But surely they wouldn't touch the Red Cross," Neville said.

"I wouldn't run in that scrimmage," the guards' commander answered, looking at the menacing mob and then at the Malaysian guards, who rolled their eyes in apprehension.

"I wouldn't either," I said, but Jim was already loading the injured man onto a stretcher.

"We'll do it," Jim muttered, clenching his pipe at a strident angle.

Leaving the others, I started to push the crowd back down the beach, which was jammed from the guards' compound past the fresh-water tanks and the hospital to the supply warehouse. Arms outstretched, my voice low and even, I paced slowly up and down in front of the crowd.

"Move on back, now," I said in Vietnamese. "Move on back."

"But they're VC!" the men protested. One tried to run past me. I grabbed his forearm and spun him around.

The little boy named Vũ, his masklike face contorted, yanked my shirt. He hardly came to my waist. "They killed my father!" He yelled over the mob's angry shouts.

"If you kill your brothers," I answered, "whom will you live with?"

I paced between the fresh-water tanks and the sea as I herded the men back to the main path. A Malaysian guard arrived. He was skittery, but together we pushed back the men who sneaked around us, laughing and chanting, "Get the VC! Get the VC!"

The guard disappeared as soon as we reached the main path; the crowd began to slip by me. Then Jim and Neville were coming down the beach, carrying a stretcher with the injured man. The other eight suspects straggled behind.

"Kill them!" the crowd roared.

The mob boiled over. Men and boys swirled around the stretcher, grabbing at the man with the bloody head, beating at him and yelling, "Kill him! Kill him!" Jim and Neville fended them off with feet and elbows. I ran in circles around the stretcher, which rocked, jostling the man with the bloody head. Jim and Neville scrambled up the steps and ran with the stretcher through the jetty gate. The other suspects raced behind. I slammed the gate into the mob.

"Enough!" I shouted. But men running in the water along-side the jetty grabbed two of the prisoners by the ankles. They ripped them off the jetty and into the water where they pounded them with fists and sandals. They pushed their heads under the water and held them there, shouting and kicking.

I jumped off the jetty and pulled at arms, elbows, fists. One suspect lay slumped over in the water. I lifted him by the waist. A Malaysian guard reached down from the jetty, but the distance was too great. The men in the water pressed closer, their shouts vicious. I squatted and, grabbing the man around the buttocks, lifted him like a sack of oats; the guard on the jetty snatched him up by the armpits. I pulled the other suspect from under the water, shook him and lifted him up.

I climbed onto a submerged boat, its deck slippery under-foot, and the guard hauled me up onto the jetty. I'd lost my flip-flops, headscarf, and pen. My watch ticked on but its expansion band had broken. Sopping clothes clung to my body. My black satin *quần* were ripped across the front thigh; ripped in the back, they hung down like the flap on a child's pajamas. Standing alone on the jetty, I watched the Malay-sian guard and the two water-soaked prisoners run toward the waiting boat.

In my room I changed into a clean pair of *quần* and found my moccasins, which the rats had fringed with teeth marks.

I've had it, I thought. I'm shipping out. But there was no boat leaving.

A heaviness began to press on me. I wanted to be else-where, anywhere else but on that island and in that stark room with its cell-like walls and its louvered windows with bars made of glass.

I wanted to be home alone in the valley with the hills rising and falling like an old cloak around me, their woods and meadows varied in texture like a favorite garment's un-evenly worn fabric. I wanted the warmth of the farm kitchen bathed in yellow light, its floor as uneven as the hills, and I wanted the comfort of the old blue rocker I'd once pulled from a friend's rubbish heap. I'd sit there and choose a book from one of the piles of kitchen clutter and let myself be buoyed like a boat in some mysterious harbor until I'd look down and see my dogs lying at my feet, their somber gazes anchoring me.

But even in memory I couldn't reach home that afternoon. I left my room. There was only one place where I knew I'd find solitude.

I walked along the beach, but didn't look up at the milling crowd left from the mob. Even when I heard my name, I kept walking. Crossing the main sewer, I climbed Religious Hill. Outside the pagoda, I stopped at the small altar I'd visited during Tết to *xin xâm*—ask for a propitious future. The spectators had laughed then, telling me to shake the bamboo container harder so that my wish would come true. Now, the golden Buddha looked forlorn with its chipped paint and part of an ear missing. Its lips were cracked as if parched; its eyes were open but empty.

I sat alone on a nearby cliff overlooking the water. The endless gray of the sea stretched on until it merged with an endlessly gray sky. Far below, children riding the waves on

Zone C beach laughed as the surf ground them into the sand. I felt like weeping, but instead I sat on the rocks and let the heaviness settle deeper within me.

Someone spoke my name. The voice had a Quảng Ngãi accent. Turning, I found the island's head monk hunkering on the rocks next to me. I'd always felt a special kinship with the Venerable because we'd each lived in Quảng Ngãi.

Once, in the Bidong acupuncture room, I'd watched him cauterize the temples of a young woman before inserting inch-long needles into her head. He'd shown me his scrolls, including one that depicted a huge ear with lines connecting its 161 treatment points to various organs and to the limbs. The Venerable had turned the diagram upside down and shown me how the ear, shaped like a fetus, suggests the entire human body.

Sitting near me on Religious Hill, Venerable Thích Huỳnh Tôn clasped his hands against his gray robe in the gesture of prayer. He wore tinted glasses and hadn't shaved his head for several days. "We must ask your forgiveness," he said, dipping again and again. "We're not ourselves on Bidong."

"None of us are," I said. "It's all right now."

Far below us, on Zone C beach, the children playing in the surf squealed as a large breaker crashed over them. The Venerable and I sat quietly, watching the children.

"Did you ever get to the sea when you lived in Quảng Ngãi?" he asked.

"Yes. Several times. Down at the end of the peninsula, past Buddha Mountain."

"Ah, Buddha Mountain." He adjusted his glasses and ran a hand over his bristle of hair. "I entered the novitiate there. I was seven." He smiled. "That's when I cut my hair."

Glancing at the Venerable, I remembered watching little boys in cinnamon robes tug at the well rope in the garden atop Buddha Mountain. All around, bougainvillaea climbed the monastery walls.

"I used to enjoy watching the novices in the garden," I ventured. "And sometimes," I added, "I'd go to the iron pine grove. Did you ever go there?" I was remembering how, during lulls in the fighting, the Quaker team would take a picnic to that grove, which looked eastward over the bombed rice paddies of Mỹ Lai to the South China Sea.

"Yes," the Venerable said, gazing at the restless gray water far below us. "Yes, but that's all in our past now."

We lapsed into silence. Then, bowing, the Venerable returned to the pagoda; I picked my way down between shanties to the path winding from Zone C beach to the center of the camp. I paused to buy flip-flops at the same stall Tú, Khanh, Vũ, and I had visited the day before. The vendor would not accept my damp ringgit; her husband insisted on fixing my watch band.

I stopped at the Coconut Inn. Before I could sit down, Flower was beside me with a cup of her brew. "Bring me those *quần*," she said, even though I hadn't mentioned the incident on the beach. "I'll mend them."

"It's useless, Flower. They're rags now."

"Bring them," she said gently, "I can sew."

After I left the Inn, strangers stopped me all along the path back to the hospital. "The VC are cruel," they told me.

"We are all cruel," I said.

🌀 16
An Island on the Island

"Have you seen the baby?" everyone was asking.

We took turns peering into an incubator donated the week before by the New Zealand Embassy. It was the size of a hamster cage and had two access holes in the front of its clear plastic shield. Inside lay a three-months-premature baby who weighed two pounds. She was diapered in a four-by-four-inch square of gauze.

The day after the incubator baby was born, I received word that Sister Christ wanted to see me in the hospital. "Is it about the baby?" I asked Small Boy, who'd brought the message. He stood leaning against the door frame, looking straight at me out of his wide eyes, one dusty foot crossed over the instep of the other.

When I entered the delivery room, I was surprised to see that Chris looked pale and drawn. Her uniform was rumpled, with spots on the skirt. She brushed her blond hair out of her eyes, which looked gray instead of the usual blue.

"I've had it," she said, her clipped voice sodden. "I can't go all night long, then run all day. Do you think you could help me feed this baby?"

"Me? Feed a baby?"

I never voluntarily hold a baby. Infants bore me when they're contented; they terrify me when they're squalling. A week earlier, a missionary journalist had insisted, despite my protests, on photographing a Vietnamese baby in my arms. When he left, all three of us—mother, child, and myself—cursed him in our separate languages. My brothers say I've always been this way about babies. They say when I was six or seven, I announced that the world already had too many people and that they could make more if they wanted to, but I'd look after the ones who needed extra tending.

"Come," Sister Christ said, pulling my sleeve. "I'll show you how to scrub."

"But it'll be a disaster, Chris. I don't know anything about babies."

"You'll learn. The Vietnamese nurses are too scared and the doctors are too busy. That leaves you." She tied a gauze mask on me, led me to the sink, and showed me how to scour my arms, hands, and nails.

"This baby requires feeding every two hours," she said.

"Sure," I said. "Whatever you say."

"I call her my beak baby."

"How's that?"

"You'll see."

I slipped my hands through the plastic shield of the incubator, and the next thing I knew I was lifting the baby into my palm. My fingers felt thick and clumsy as if I were wearing boxing gloves. The infant had soft, loose skin covered with gentle down, and her ears were pressed into her head. She was the size of a dove and she had a mouth that opened and closed like the featherless baby birds my brothers and I had tried unsuccessfully to feed with eyedroppers.

"See?" Sister Christ whispered beside me. "A beak baby."

The infant lay waiting in my left palm. Her mouth opened, gaping. Every time I brought the syringe down close to her lips, she kicked my wrist, shattering my aim. Her tiny fists beat at the syringe, making me jerk its plunger. The milk spurted; she gagged. I was terrified I'd drowned her.

"Lift her head a little," Chris said. Her voice was low and steady.

I raised my left wrist and dropped my fingers slightly so that the infant was almost sitting. A cough rose from a hollow deep in my chest. I stifled it, but the vibrations broke through in shivers of sweat that trickled from my armpits down my forearms and into the incubator. My back ached as, squinting through the plastic, I counted one-two-three drops and waited as the beak baby swallowed.

"That's enough or you really will drown her," Chris said. "Now, the other end."

Peering through plastic, I removed the gauze diaper. Gingerly I wiped the infant with a cotton swab. I removed the damp sheet and urged a clean one under her head, shoulders, and buttocks. Carefully I tucked a new four-by-four-inch gauze square between her thighs and laid the child on her side. Her tiny chest rose and fell. I closed the incubator doors and checked the temperature and oxygen. On the far side of the room I removed my mask, wiping sweat from my chin and wrists. There, at a distance from the baby, who'd already fallen asleep, I let the nervous cough rack me.

When she was five days old, the beak baby was named Julie Andrews. Now, her father, Toàn, also fed her. He was in his early twenties, and had bristly hair and skin stretched tautly over his face, accenting his high cheekbones. In Saigon he had made his living as a musician. On Bidong he led a band called Nhạc Trẻ or Young Sound, which performed American country and popular songs over the loudspeakers every Thursday evening. His drum set, made from ration tins and water jugs, was the envy of all the island's musicians.

In performance Toàn could belt out a song's finale with such vigor that no one would doubt his determination. Off-stage he was shy and quiet. Late at night, when he fed his baby daughter, a procedure that took a good half hour, he placed the lyrics to "My Way" on top of the incubator and in a heavily accented voice softly practiced:

I've lived a life that's full
I've traveled each and every highway
And more, much more than this,
I did it my way.

He sang those words over and over, memorizing them as he waited for Julie Andrews to swallow.

One day as I was stroking Julie Andrews's chin after giving her milk, I heard screams that made my bones rattle. I closed the incubator and went to the general ward. A Vietnamese doctor was cleaning out a woman's foot, which had swollen to double size until the skin looked as if it would burst. The foot was red and purple and gray and black and smelled of rotten meat.

The woman twisted against the straps binding her to a hospital trolley. As I leaned over her, she beat her fists against my back and tore at my shirt. She smelled of rancid sweat. For perhaps a half hour I held onto her while she screamed and the doctor continued his work.

"Why didn't you use anesthesia?" I asked him afterward, struggling to contain my anger. Some of the Vietnamese doctors would prescribe an IV drip for a stubbed toe but no pain-killer for minor surgery.

"We didn't use it for that kind of surgery during the war," he answered.

"But the war's over. We've got a room full of the stuff. Please, please use it."

Later, in the Coconut Inn, I spoke with Neville. "Could you take responsibility for her?" I'd been disturbed by the doctor's technique as well as by his failure to administer any anesthetic.

And so it was that Mrs. Foot, as Neville called her, came to be his patient. Three weeks earlier, she had stepped on a splinter shortly after her boat had landed on a mainland beach. She had walked ten miles before MRCS staff picked up her and her fellow passengers and brought them to Bidong.

"Shine it a little to the left," Neville said as I aimed a flashlight directly into the hole in Mrs. Foot's arch. It was midafternoon. We had planned to look into the foot first thing that morning but had been delayed by a case of infectious meningitis, a second tetanus case in advanced stages of muscular spasms and two new cases of whooping cough. "Now down a little." Neville had drawn a screen to cordon off the gawkers from Mrs. Foot's bed. He hadn't wanted to contaminate the operating room with the germs rampant in her wound.

"Pass the scalpel. No, the other one." He poked at the hole in the bottom of the foot, scraping and cutting until his fingers poked right up through the foot and out the top. I struggled not to gag. "You have to be ruthless with dead tissue, absolutely ruthless," he said as he cut and scraped. "You have to be ruthless," he said over and over.

Mrs. Foot was awake. A look of terror had replaced the pain of the day before.

"Now what do you think about those toes?" Neville said, talking to himself. He was cutting from the center of the foot directly up to the crevice between the big toe and the second. His movements were quick and expert. "Do you think we might be able to save the ball of her foot?"

Mrs. Foot's face contorted. "Too long, doctor, too long," she gasped. "I'm dead already." With her hands she ripped at her hair. She bit her lip until it bled.

"Looking better, looking better," Neville murmured. He attached a clear peroxide drip that ran into the top of the foot and dribbled from the bottom into a basin. The liquid in the basin was a gray-red.

As Neville was cleaning up, I dabbed Tiger Balm onto Mrs. Foot's temples and below her nose. Her nostrils flared. She took the vial from me and touched the green oil to the corners of my eyes and to the furrow in my upper lip: my eyes watered and my nose burned, seared by the pungent fragrance. My head cleared of the stench of rot.

In the evening, when I stopped by to check on Mrs. Foot, she was sitting up in bed, her leg propped over the tin basin. Her grandson, Ry, slept curled next to her. Ten years old, he fetched her food and emptied her bedpan. Mrs. Foot was laughing, high on a pain-killer Neville had given her.

The next day Neville and Chris anesthetized Mrs. Foot with a nerve block at the ankle. Once more Neville cut into her wound. He reconnected the peroxide drip and bandaged her up again. Mrs. Foot's end of the general ward smelled of decay.

In the afternoon, two delegates from the League of Red Cross Societies followed Chris and me into Mrs. Foot's ward. They came to the island for two hours every month to advise on program matters. Both men wore tight jeans and their bellies pushed out against their cowboy shirts. Each carried a can of soda. They'd been hanging over us, making lewd jokes as they touched the under side of our upper arms.

"Don't you ever change that bandage?" the delegate from the Balkan peninsula asked condescendingly.

"When does their boat leave?" Chris whispered.

"Look," the delegate from central Europe said to me, "we want to show you something." They set their empty cola cans on Mrs. Foot's window sill and led me out of the hospital and onto the main path. We walked past the afternoon market with its smuggled apples and its bread fresh from oil-drum ovens until we reached the main sewer, which was as wide as a road and as deep as I am tall. Soda cans, cigarette butts, ration wrappers, and rat carcasses lay in its green ooze.

"Look at that mess," the delegate from central Europe said.

"It's a sewer," I said.

"Tho. Isn't that his name? The toothy doctor that laughs all the time. He seems reasonable for a Vietnamese. Why don't you get him to clean this up?"

You overstuffed rodent, I thought. Why don't you go clean your plate in some chic restaurant?

"Sure," I said pleasantly, nodding over my rage. "Good idea. Tomorrow we'll get right on it."

Within a half hour I was sending the delegates off with smiles and waves. I hated myself for this duplicity, but I badly needed the oxygen they would send for Julie Andrews.

That evening, when I went in to check on Mrs. Foot, I deposited in the rubbish bin the cola cans the delegates had left behind. "They took the meat and left me the bones," Mrs. Foot said, laughing loudly at her own joke. She was high again on Neville's pain-killer.

When she was strong enough, Julie Andrews's mother took over my shifts feeding and changing. Several years younger than Toàn, Lan was a demure woman who looked at her feet when she spoke. She and Toàn had met when they came to Bidong on the same boat. Like all the islanders, they lacked nationality; legally they could not marry, have children, or, for that matter, die.

One midnight when I came into the room where we kept Julie Andrews, Lan was standing before the incubator. Julie Andrews was two and a half weeks old. Through the shield holes Lan stroked her daughter's tiny chin to make the mouth open.

"Each day a little weaker," she said.

"Yes."

"She's not breathing." Lan's voice was soft.

"Tap the chest," I said.

I, too, was leaning over the incubator. With the back of my fingers I stroked Lan's shoulder. She touched the baby's chest and waited. Then with a syringe she fed another millimeter of her breast milk and lay Julie Andrews on her side. The tiny infant's chest rose and fell.

While on Bidong, I received through the mail a small carving covered with fleece, a sheep with a black face. It had been sent by a close friend in the States. I placed the sheep next to the dictionaries on my shelf.

Vietnamese children who came into my room would look first at the snapshots of the valley and of the kids who rode my bus. They would pick up the conch shell Uncle had found on Zone C beach and hold it next to one ear. Then, sucking in their breath, they would pause and, taking down the sheep, pet its wool. Pulling a curl, they giggled when it sprang back. Invariably they lifted the tail and peeked.

Of all my friends, the person to hold the sheep most gently was Kim, the towhead boy whom the other children called "American" even though he spoke no English. Standing on the jetty, I often heard my name and looked out over the dark bodies of swimming children to see Kim's golden head, alone.

One night when Kim was in my room, he took the sheep down with both hands. He stood it on his palm and touched the fur with his forefinger. Gently he raised the tail. He gazed at me with his gray-blue eyes, and with both hands lifted the carving back onto the shelf.

A week after his visit, when I heard the jetty megaphone calling Kim's name for departure, I took down the carving and laid it in a tin box with red Chinese characters painted on the lid. I tucked supply-pink toilet paper around the legs and over the wool, closed the tin, and ran with it downstairs to the jetty.

One evening I was typing a medical report when I heard a tap at the door. I opened it to find Khanh standing dwarfed in his pajama shirt, his face expectant. Then he was gone. By the time I reached the balcony, Khanh was running down the beach, calling Tú and Vũ. They all came bounding up the stairs, two at a time.

With our arms around each other the four of us leaned over the balcony railing. It was almost dark. Below, children swarmed over a newly arrived boat beached on the sand, laughing as they chased each other around the decks. In the cabin, three boys vied for the steering wheel. Jabbing with elbows, they shoved each other aside.

The light faded until we could no longer see the boys clearly. The boat and the children on deck, the jetty and those who sat there talking darkened into black shapes silhouetted against deep purple. The voices of the people on the beach faded and the sounds of the waves rose. We looked out over the sea at a semicircle of lights and beyond the lights, the mountains of mainland Malaysia jagged against the sky.

"What are the lights?" Tú asked. She could speak clearly now.

"Fishing boats." I was stroking her hair, which no longer felt stiff with salt. I felt her body tense. "Malay fishing boats," I said, "not Thai pirates."

From my pocket I removed four peppermints. We twisted off the papers, which crackled, and popped the candies into our mouths. The peppermint tasted sharp.

"I'm terrified," Tú said as our tongues worked the candy, "terrified of the sea."

"I can still taste that child's mouth," Chris said. We were sitting in the front of the Land-Rover, and she was driving. We were on the way to the Trengganu Hospital morgue.

Earlier in the day, Chris and the assistant surgeon had loaded a seven-year-old onto the midday boat. The child had been playing in her blue plastic hut when a palm tree fell on it, impaling her abdomen on a bamboo spike from the hut's table. For an hour after the child stopped breathing, Chris and the doctor took turns trying to resuscitate her. After they reached the mainland, they called on the radio, saying that the girl was dead. I accompanied the parents to Trengganu on the UN speedboat. The three of us rode together on the bow, the wind whipping the father's thick hair into his face. With his shoulders he protected his weeping wife from the spray.

In the Trengganu morgue we said prayers for the child whose face was fresh and round, framed by soft hair in a Dutch boy cut. Hospital attendants loaded her into a small box made of rough lumber. The mother tucked rags around her daughter's shoulders and under her head. She waited while the father nailed the lid, wincing at each of his blows. When he finished, she rubbed her fingers over the lid the way one might stroke a child's forehead.

We drove through darkness to the paupers' cemetery. I sat in the back with the parents, our feet pulled up under us so as not to step on the coffin. At the cemetery we waited for the gravediggers. Lightning flashed, illuminating the grave mounds. Only scrub brush grew around them. Soon, a motorcycle carrying two men with shovels wove between the graves. The cycle swerved and the wheels spat sand at the nearby mounds. The driver stopped and gunned his engine.

A full moon hazed by rain silhouetted the gravediggers as they sliced their shovels into the sand. The sand made a whisking sound as it flew off their spades. Raindrops pattered against the canvas top of the Land-Rover. Inside, the mother leaned over and rested her cheek on the coffin lid. As soon as I saw the gravediggers approaching, I touched her shoulder.

The men slid the box out of the Land-Rover and lowered it into the hole. When the coffin tilted, lob-ended, one of the gravediggers leaped onto it and jumped up and down. Furious, I stifled my anger and suggested he pry with a shovel. I was squatting beside the grave and next to the mother. Rain spotted her tattered blouse. It trickled down the back of my neck.

Hunkering like children on a beach, we began to push sand

into the hole. The sand felt cool and gritty. The father pulled
off a branch of scrub brush and planted it at the head of the
grave as the mother and I patted the cold outside layer of
sand.

During my last two months on Bidong, I made many trips
to the mainland. Always, when I returned, Tú and Khanh and
Vũ were waiting for me at the end of the jetty. Sometimes
they were joined by Ry, who was Mrs. Foot's grandson, or by
Thúy Hẳng, who'd brought water to Mai when she was delirious.

Vũ, whose sunburned eye sockets had healed, no longer
looked quite so much like a raccoon. He had worked out an
arrangement with a baker to sell donuts, two for one ringgit.
The donuts were heavy and scant on sugar, but palatable if
warm. Tú and Khanh sold pigs' ears, sweet crackers made
from coconut dough rolled thin and deep-fat-fried. When
cooled, they were as addictive as potato chips. Full of chatter,
Tú would hand me a fistful of pigs' ears as soon as I'd signed in
with the Malaysian jetty guard.

"How's Julie Andrews?" I'd ask. I always feared the answer.

"Fine," Tú would say. "Though sometimes she forgets to
breathe."

"The Vietnamese fishermen caught a giant sea turtle!"
Khanh was bursting to talk when I returned from one trip.
He'd long since discarded his pajama shirt; his chest was
deeply tanned.

"Huge!" Tú said, laughing. "As big as a boat!"

"Bigger!" Vũ said, bugging his raccoon eyes.

"They threw it back, I hope." I'd heard about those leath-
erback turtles. Several yards in length, they nested only in

Trengganu State and two other places in the world. They were sacred to Malays.

"Oh no! The fishermen kept it," Thúy Hằng said. She shook her head, and the tiny gold hoops in her ears swayed. "They cut it up and sold it on the market."

My heart turned over. There'd be trouble.

"Then there was the fire!" Khanh had taken my briefcase as we walked toward the hospital.

Ry was dancing with excitement. "The Malaysian guards took all the Vietnamese fishing boats and burned them! A hundred boats. A bonfire!" He pointed down the beach to the Malaysian compound. Trouble had long since arrived. Malaysian guards, enraged at the destruction of the inviolable turtle, scowled at a pile of glowing embers, all that was left from a fleet of dinghies the islanders had made from pilfered plywood.

"And your grandmother?" I asked Ry. "How is she?"

"See for yourself."

I looked over and saw Mrs. Foot sitting at a hospital window, her leg propped up, a crutch nearby. Neville had been able to save the foot, even the toes. Now she could move about on crutches, her oozing bandage wrapped in a ration bag. She waved from the window and laughed—this time without pain-killers. Even on the beach below, I could hear her.

⊗ 17

Home

The tide was running out. The surf broke across mud flats and rippled against boat hulls with that lapping sound I remembered from my childhood, when I would curl in my bunk against *Erma*'s side. Chatting with the MRCS staff on the warehouse beach, I could smell brine and mud and cabbages as I lifted a coffee jar of wine to my lips.

Sister Christ returned from feeding Julie Andrews, as Uncle, sitting like a Buddha before tiers of rations, complained about yet another shipment of rotting cabbages. We all sniffed the air and nodded our acknowledgment. A rat scampered into our circle and paused, nose quivering, before it scurried into the warehouse. Selva poured more wine into instant-coffee jars and we spoke of Monika's departure for Frankfurt that morning, of Jim's for Bangladesh the week before, and of mine in three days.

Those few moments together, as soothing as the lapping of the sea on mossy hulls, comprised my farewell with the MRCS staff.

The next afternoon I missed Julie Andrews's one-month birthday celebration, which took place across the hall in Monika's room, where Sister Christ now lived. Sitting at my desk, I could hear genteel conversation over tea and pigs' ears as I translated for a UN official an islander's story about fifteen thousand American dollars' worth of diamonds. A man had peered over the woman's gunnysack wall late one night while she counted her jewels. The next night he cut a hole in the gunnysack and anesthetized her before he removed the jewels from her vagina, where she had stored them.

One day my last week on the island, a Vietnamese worker from the Administration Division pulled me off the main path. I knew her casually from processing new arrivals in the Malaysian guards' compound. She lifted her long, thick hair from her neck as she asked for my birth date and my date of arrival on Bidong. Laughing, she chalked these onto a square of plywood. Onlookers gathered, chuckling as she added my boat number, *RC 2*.

"Name?" she asked.

"Lý," I answered.

"Family name?"

I hesitated. "Borton."

Someone hissed. The other spectators laughed.

"Oh no!" the young woman said. "That won't do at all. You must have a Vietnamese family name. If you like, you could take mine, 'Nguyễn.' It belongs to the royal family."

"And to most of the rest of us," said a man with a dragon tattooed on his arm.

"Make it 'Nguyễn' then," I said. " 'Nguyễn thị Lý.' " I added a customary middle name for women.

She chalked the name onto the plywood and held the

board below my chin while a man snapped my picture. Then she recorded the data on a UN identification card and, taking my thumb, rolled it on an ink pad and pressed it onto the card.

"There," she said, tossing her luxuriant hair, "that makes you officially one of us."

As I left the Administration Division, a stranger stopped me. His golden skin was pockmarked with shrapnel scars. In his hands he carried his ration book.

"Where did you learn to speak?" he asked. From his Vietnamese tones I could tell that his background was rural.

"In Quảng Ngãi."

"I think you lived there in 1970."

I blinked in surprise.

"You wore black *quần* and Vietnamese rubber tire sandals. On Sundays you used to walk alone to the market."

I nodded.

"Quảng Ngãi is my *quê hưởng*. I remember seeing you in the market. You were buying pineapples."

When I returned from Quảng Ngãi in 1971, the memories of Vietnamese hung about me like a shroud. Yet Americans didn't want to hear about the war.

Perhaps to heal ourselves, most of us who'd worked with the Quakers in Vietnam chose to live near another teammate. During the years I lived with Eric, we never probed our Quảng Ngãi experiences. Other teammates seemed to follow this same pattern. Perhaps no one—not our stateside friends or even our former teammates—knew the questions to ask; more likely, we didn't have the words to answer.

I do remember one exception. I think it was in the fall of 1971. I was walking down the steps of the Capitol, where I had been lobbying. A handsome, bearded man stopped me and asked if we'd met before. I felt peeved at that flirtatious line, but then a playful earnestness in his eyes seemed familiar. I sorted back through faces until I came to the years I'd taught in a Quaker boarding school, where a beardless boy with those same eyes watched me from the second row of my first algebra class. I could still remember his exhausting persistence over the binomial theorem and that it had been he who'd badgered me into chaperoning the 1965 Pentagon protest against the Marines' landing in Đànẵng. That vigil had led me to other protests and eventually, four years later, to Vietnam.

As Rick and I paused on the steps, the afternoon sun softened the white Capitol dome to ivory and reflected off the bronze statue of Freedom raising her sword. We sat down as Rick began to speak about his work on Native American Indian rights with the Quaker lobby across the street. Together we reminisced about acquaintances in common. When Rick asked about Vietnam, his tone was earnest and his eyes were a gentle brown. I talked about Vietnamese friends whose voices I still heard. I hunted words for Rick.

We talked until the congressional staff came down the steps and until spotlights illumined the bronze statue atop the dome. Then we shook hands and hugged and went our separate ways. That was the last news I heard of Rick until some months later, when I learned that he'd left his work with the Quaker lobby to join the team in Quảng Ngãi. He died there.

The day before I left Bidong, Vũ and Khanh took me swimming on Zone C beach. The other children looked down at their own batik brown bodies and then laughed at me. "She has the whiteness of terror," said a little girl, who was wearing around her neck a pouch of herbs to ward off evil spirits.

I swam way out, enjoying the motion of my body through water. Pausing, I looked back over the children splashing in the waves. Then as I lay back, the sea filtered out the voices and the rasp of loudspeakers. I gazed up at the mountain streaked with landslides and peppered with stumps; I rolled over and peered at fish slipping through fingers of coral.

Later I sat on the hospital balcony with Sister Christ and Peter, the new doctor who'd replaced Neville. We watched the evening shift from blue to orange until the water shimmered with the sky and the skeletal hulls seemed to burn. Below us, people gathered, sitting on the jetty and on abandoned boats where they, too, chatted as they watched the day fade. Friends waved to us; children ran up the staircase. Tú and Vũ leaned against the railing; Khanh climbed into my lap and sat there, petting the hair on my arms.

Bạch came by my room. During the war, he had advanced through Saigon Navy ranks to earn a year's study of logistics in Rhode Island, which he remembered as a land of opportunity. His wife, who'd never traveled, looked toward the States with fear. Bạch hadn't heard from his American sponsor, yet he couldn't leave the island without that sponsor's assurance of support. I agreed to check the sponsorship and, if need be, to initiate the papers so that Bạch and his wife could leave Bidong for the Ohio hills.

"You're half Vietnamese, I think," Bạch said in English as he pulled on the lone hair curling like a question mark from the mole on his chin.

"Perhaps," I replied in Vietnamese, "just as you're half American. And neither of us will ever feel whole in either country."

That night I attended a joint farewell party for Thọ and myself, a formal affair in the new outpatient clinic. Afterward

I sat alone in my room, stripped of its clutter, and looked at the snapshots I'd taken down from the wall over my desk. The kids on my bus smiled through Bidong dust; teeth marks fringed a photo of the valley in July haze. Replacing the snapshots in my briefcase, I felt as if Bidong had cured me of a long, painful illness. I was ready to go back to America.

I glanced through the window louvers into the darkness. Two or three people passed along the beach below, their conversation only a murmur. Loudspeakers in a palm outside the window began playing the farewell song aired the night before each movement.

Ngày mai em đi
Biển nhớ tên em gọi về . . .

Hôm nao em về
Bàn tay buông lối ngõ
Đàn lên cung phím chờ
Sầu lên dây hoang vu.

Tomorrow you'll leave
Oceans of yearning call you back . . .

Some day you'll return
With hands hanging down in the old way
Music will cast its waiting net
Tuning the plaintive strings.

Sadness washed over me. I was the only one leaving the next day. They were playing that song for me.

The next morning Tú stopped by my room. I gave her the tiny box filled with the dove necklace that had hung over my desk until rats swung on it. She restrung the necklace as I packed. Then she led me to the jetty, where I moved through the crowd, clasping hands. There was Thọ, who promised to beat me to Ohio; Big and Little Hửng, the new heads of the Health Division; Dục, the camp leader who'd divided three tons of raw fish; Bạch; Selva, Uncle, and Sister Christ; Julie Andrews's parents; Flower; and Tú wearing her dove.

And then there was Bạch again. I couldn't look into his sorrowful eyes, I couldn't speak or even reach for his hand. Suddenly I felt some long protected part of me begin to quiver and feared that there, surrounded by my friends, I would cry.

I leaped into the idling UN speedboat. The captain yanked the throttle, and the speedboat arched away from the jetty, its engines drowning out the farewell shouts. Hanging onto the boat's railing, my hair snapping in the wind, my eyes smarting, I watched the faces and waving hands until they became indistinguishable from the jetty. The pier and Religious Hill with its clinging blue houses receded until the camp shrank behind a curve of sea foam, and all I could see was Bidong's volcanic cone thrusting from the sea.

I sat alone in the stern of the UN launch, holding on my lap the conch shell Uncle had found on Zone C beach. The conch was pink and curved, smooth and fluted like an ear. From its core twined delicate lines like staffs of music. Without lifting that shell, I knew its weight, and without listening, I knew that it harbored, at the center of its spiral, the sound of voices.